Wildcat Aces
of World War 2

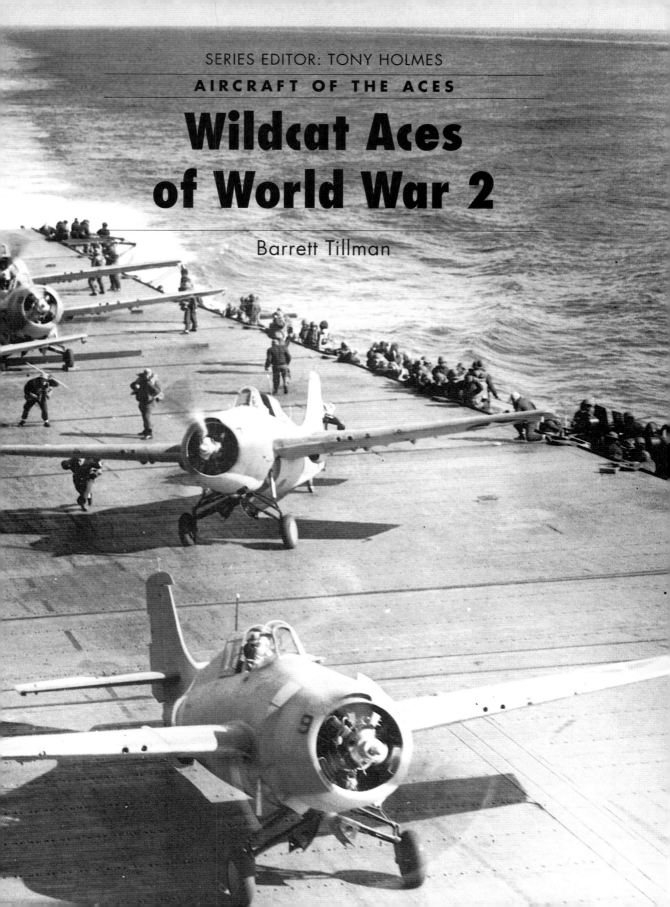

SERIES EDITOR: TONY HOLMES

AIRCRAFT OF THE ACES

Wildcat Aces
of World War 2

Barrett Tillman

Front cover
With hunter-like precision, Capt Joe Foss of VMF-121 fires a short burst from his F4F-4's six .50 cal Brownings into a second Mitsubishi G4M1 'Betty' of the Misawa Naval Air Group. Below him, a mortally damaged 'Betty' glides down towards 'The Slot', off Guadalcanal, the bomber also a victim of Foss' deadly accurate fire. This action took place on 18 October 1942, Foss having already claimed two Zeros destroyed and a third damaged earlier in the sortie whilst fighting his way through to the bombers – he was now an ace, and he had only been at Henderson Field nine days!
(Cover Painting by Iain Wyllie)

First published in Great Britain in Spring 1995
by Osprey, an imprint of Reed International Books
Michelin House, 81 Fulham Road,
London SW3 6RB
and Auckland, Melbourne

Reprinted winter 1995, 1997

ISBN 1 85532 486 5

Edited by Tony Holmes
Design by TT Designs, Tony & Stuart Truscott

Cover Artwork by Iain Wyllie
Aircraft Profiles by Chris Davey, Keith Fretwell and John Weal
Aircraft Profiles Text by Jon Lake
Figure Artwork by Mike Chappell
Scale Drawings by Mark Styling

Printed in China

ACKNOWLEDGEMENTS
The editor would like to thank Capt Eric Brown CBE, DSC, AFC, RN, and his wife, for their warm hospitality and generosity in providing both memories and photographs for this volume. Thanks also to Phil Jarrett, Robert L Lawson, Jon Lake, Jerry Scutts and Richard Riding at *Aeroplane* for the provision of other key photographs.

CONTENTS

PRE-WAR NAVAL AVIATION AND EARLY CAMPAIGNS

When the United States Navy went to general quarters in December 1941, its aviation branch was a weapon in transition. The last carrier-based biplanes had barely disappeared, as USS *Yorktown's* (CV-5) fighter squadron had only recently transitioned from Grumman F3F-3s to monoplane F4F-3 Wildcats.

The Wildcat was a leading-edge aircraft in its day. Powered by a Pratt & Whitney R-1830-76 radial engine, the F4F-3 was only the third monoplane to enter fleet service in the US Navy. The -3A model, produced in smaller numbers, had the R-1830-90 engine with a single-stage, two-speed, supercharger. Both engines were rated at 1200 horsepower and both aircraft models had 'stiff' (non-folding) wings bearing four Browning .50 cal machine guns.

At the time of Pearl Harbor the Navy had seven carriers in commission, three of which were assigned to the Pacific Fleet in Hawaii. In fact, on 7 December USS *Lexington* (CV-2) was ferrying Marine Corps scout-bombers to Midway while *Enterprise* (CV-6) had just delivered a Marine fighter squadron to Wake Island. *Saratoga* (CV-3), meanwhile, was embarking her air group in San Diego, California, while also loading another Marine fighter unit.

On the East Coast *Yorktown* faced a minor crisis. Her assigned fighter squadron, VF-5, was temporarily on neutrality patrol, so she hastily embarked a *Ranger* (CV-4) squadron – VF-42 – then steamed for the Pacific. *Ranger* herself was the first US carrier laid down as such from the word go, and was unsuited for the vast Pacific Ocean theatre – she spent most of the war with the Atlantic Fleet. Two newer carriers, *Wasp* (CV-7) and *Hornet* (CV-8), were also based on the East Coast, but would eventually fall victim to the Imperial Japanese Navy.

Despite somewhat different aircraft types (*Lexington* still flew Brewster Buffalos rather than Wild-

The father of all Wildcats, Grumman's prototype XF4F BuNo 0383 was progressively modified over a period of two years from the date of its first flight on 2 September 1937 until it appeared in a configuration close to that adopted by production F4F-3s in late 1939. This particular shot shows the aircraft in its transitional phase in early 1939 *(via Phil Jarrett)*

Newly-received F4F-3s of *Ranger's* VF-42 taxy for take-off from NAS Norfolk, Virginia, in the spring of 1941. The nearest aircraft is 42-F-8, featuring an aluminium fuselage, green tail and chrome-yellow wings. The BuNo on the vertical stabiliser is 2527, which makes this F4F only the 67th production Wildcat ever built *(via Robert L Lawson)*

cats), each US Navy carrier embarked a well-balanced air group of four squadrons. With the exception of *Ranger* and *Wasp*, which boasted two VF units apiece, each ship carried two squadrons of Douglas SBD-2/3 Dauntlesses, a Douglas TBD-1 Devastator torpedo squadron and an F4F-3/3A 'FitRon' (Fighter Squadron). Nominal strength of each unit was 18 aircraft, plus an SBD for the air group commander, or CAG. Contrary to some accounts, each prewar air group was identified by its ship rather than the carrier's hull number. *Lexington*, for instance, was CV-2; she flew the Lexington Air Group, rather than Air Group Two, but all her squadrons bore that numeral (VB-2, VF-2, VS-2 and VT-2). The first numbered air groups that were not originally affiliated with a particular carrier only appeared in mid-1942.

The Wildcat was still relatively new in fleet service. Barely a year before, in November 1940, Fighting Squadron Four had received the initial batch of production F4F-3s from Grumman's Bethpage, New York, factory. However, by this stage the Royal Navy's Fleet Air Arm (FAA) was already operating its first truly modern fighters – Grumman G-36A export models originally ordered by the French *Aéronavale*. When Germany invaded France in the summer of 1940, the G-36s were delivered to Britain instead, where they were redesignated Martlet Is.

In December 1941 the US Navy possessed nine fighting squadrons ('fighter' was a postwar term) and the Marine Corps four. Of these, one Navy and one Marine unit flew Brewster F2A-3 Buffalos; the rest were either operational with F4F-3s and -3As, or re-equipping with them.

At the time of Pearl Harbor the Navy counted 131 Wildcats in operational squadrons: 103 in the Atlantic Fleet and 29 with the Pacific. Two Marine Corps squadrons in Virginia and one in Hawaii numbered 61 F4Fs, while another two-dozen or so resided in fleet pools and miscellaneous commands. However, the Navy F4F squadrons faced a serious deficit, with only 48 per cent of their authorised aircraft on strength – Grumman production was struggling to catch up with allotments. Ironically, the Marines (long accustomed to taking a back seat) actually showed a surplus, with 112 per cent of authorised strength.

Organization among F4F units was no different from other carrier squadrons. Wildcats were divided into three or four divisions, usually led by the commanding officer, executive officer and flight (operations) officer, respectively. However, by late 1941 a doctrinal shift was gaining momentum in naval fighter circles. Dating from the biplane era, three-aircraft sections and six-aircraft divisions were still employed in most Wildcat and Buffalo squadrons. But combat experience from Europe showed a trend toward two-fighter sections and four-fighter divisions (respectively termed 'elements' and 'flights' in the Army Air Force). The advantage derived from this tactical change was greater flexibility and a net increase in combat effectiveness, for two pair of leaders and wingmen held greater initiative than two trios. In the dynamic, high-speed, world

Bearing early-war markings, VF-72's 'Fox 14' is salvaged after a landing incident at Pungo Airfield, North Carolina. The two-tone grey colour scheme is evident, as is the unusual rendering of the side number – 72F14 – without the usual hyphens separating the squadron number, type and individual aircraft. VF-72 flew from its parent carrier, USS *Wasp*, until she was sunk in September 1942, then fought much of the Solomons campaign from *Hornet*, and ashore on Guadalcanal – the unit's tally for 1942 was 38 kills. Six aces flew with VF-72, but only Ens G L Wrenn scored five victories whilst assigned to the unit *(via Robert L Lawson)*

Following an effort of extreme manual dexterity, the lead pilot of this anonymous quartet of F4F-3s has managed to twist both himself and his camera around to record 'his' section proudly stacked up in echelon port formation. Photographed just months prior to the outbreak of war in August 1941, all three Wildcats wear an unusual red cross alongside their national insignia, both on the fuselage and the wings. This marking was applied for joint-service war games staged in Louisiana *(via Phil Jarrett)*

Directed by a chief petty officer, four 'whitehats' prepare to install the port wing on a VF-3 aircraft. Note the 'Felix the Cat' emblem below the windscreen – employed by various units since 1941, it has remained one of the most enduring insignia in naval aviation. Additional aircraft are stored overhead, attached to the hangar deck roof, above the SBD-2s of VS-3 and TBD-1s of VT-3. Originally based aboard *Saratoga*, these units (with VB-3) also saw combat from other carriers during 1942 *(via Robert L Lawson)*

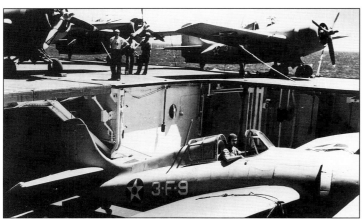

A plane captain rides 3-F-19 by elevator up to *Saratoga*'s flight deck in 1941. Other 'Fighting Three' Wildcats are already secured with wheel chocks and tie-downs. At this time the standard complement for carrier fighter squadrons was 18 aircraft and 19 or 20 pilots. However, early combat experience quickly demonstrated a need for more F4Fs, and by the Battle of Midway the number had grown to 27 F4Fs *(via Robert L Lawson)*

of aerial combat, section integrity frequently broke down, and a loner caught by a competent pair was likely to be doomed. Eventually, combat would sort out the difference, with the Japanese only following the global trend in mid-1943.

By January 1942 the US Navy and Marine Corps fighting squadrons were very much a mixture of old and new aviators. Most squadron COs and XOs were Naval Academy graduates, career officers of lieutenant or lieutenant commander rank. As a rule, they were at least 3000-hour pilots, usually with experience in a variety of aircraft types. For instance, since 1930 Lt Cdr John S Thach, who led VF-3 within the Saratoga Air Group, had served in patrol squadrons as well as fighters.

Middle-level aviators were generally lieutenants (junior grade) whose collateral duties involved supervising engineering, gunnery, navigation and other departments. However, by far the largest group of pilots within any unit held the rank of ensign. The most junior were recent graduates of NAS Pensacola, but several had as much as three years fleet experience.

Finally, the Navy (and, to a lesser extent, the Marines) possessed a cadre of non-commissioned aviators. Designated naval aviation pilots, or NAPs, the enlisted fliers were already known for a high level of competence and experience. Nearly all were commissioned in the year after Pearl Harbor, and many rose to leadership positions. However, some Annapolis-bred officers never truly adjusted to the situation and failed to make full use of their NAPs' professional skills. The programme expired upon retirement of the last serving NAPs, circa 1970.

Marine Corps F4F squadrons were virtually identical to their Navy counterparts, with one difference. While nearly all Marine aviators were carrier-qualified, no Marine squadrons regularly operated from carriers until late 1944. In part the reason was a scarcity of carriers, which became increasingly scarcer during 1942. But Marine Corps aviation was doctrinally a supporting arm of the infantry – as much as the artillery. Consequently, though several units launched off carrier decks for Guadalcanal and other climes, they flew combat from airfields in direct support of the 'mud Marines'.

CAMPAIGNS

The little Grumman's US debut on the wartime stage was inauspicious. Though FAA Martlets had shot down German aircraft as early as Christmas Day 1940, the F4F's first loss in a combat theatre with the US Navy came at friendly hands. *Enterprise* diverted six F4F-3s to Ford Island, Pearl Harbor, on the evening of 7 December, and mixed signals resulted in tragedy. Frightened and shell-shocked anti-aircraft gunners, unaware that friendly aircraft were landing, opened fire on VF-6. In the darkness and confusion, two F4Fs were shot down, and pilots bailed out of two more. Three well-trained aviators died in the shambles. Thus began the

Wildcat's status as a 'first-to-last warrior' in the Pacific arena.

Meanwhile, across the International Date Line on Wake Island, VMF-211 was bleeding the enemy in an action that remains legendary to this day. *Enterprise* had delivered Maj Paul Putnam's squadron only days before, and Wake's garrison

'air force' had hardly settled in when enemy bombers struck. Seven Wildcats were destroyed on the ground, leaving just five to confront the enemy's entire 24th Air Flotilla in the Marshall Islands. Owing to parts shortages, there were never more than four operational F4Fs, and then only briefly. In the next four days the Marine aviators claimed six enemy aircraft – four Mitsubishi G3Ms, later called 'Nells' by Allied intelligence, and a Kawanishi H6K 'Mavis'. Lt David Kliewer and Tech Sgt W J Hamilton shared the first bomber on 9 December, followed by two each on the 10th and 11th for Capt Henry Elrod and Lt C P Davidson, respectively. On that date Lt J F Kinney hit another G3M, which made off trailing smoke. The next day Capt F C Tharin splashed a flying boat

Over the next two weeks VMF-211 worked minor miracles under the direction of Lt Kinney. Cut off from all help, the Marines fought on despite severe shortages of bombs, ammunition and spare parts – even tools. By cannibalising parts from the wrecks, and by constantly improvising, VMF-211 maintained a small, but effective, resistance against enemy air and sea power. Despite dwindling resources – only two F4Fs were flyable at the end – Putnam's squadron sank two ships and claimed eight aircraft. The last aerial combat occurred on the 22nd when Japanese carrier aircraft raided Wake, and Capt H C Freuler led the interception. That mission cost one pilot and both remaining F4Fs. When the enemy seized the island on their second attempt the following morning, aviators and mechanics fought on as infantry.

By then the US Pacific Fleet had regrouped and was able to plan its first tentative steps: a series of hit-and-run raids against enemy bases. On 1 February 'The Big E' launched strikes against Kwajalein Atoll in the Marshalls. After dropping light bombs, VF-6 engaged Mitsubishi A5M 'Claudes' and Lt(jg) W E Rawie shot one down in a head-on pass. It was the first aerial victory for a carrier-based F4F, and was followed by another that afternoon as land-based bombers harried Vice Adm W F Halsey's task force.

Simultaneously, the newly-arrived *Yorktown* attempted strikes against bases in the Gilberts. Adverse weather spoiled the effort, but VF-42 nevertheless destroyed a Kawanishi flying boat near the task force that afternoon. However, these early successes were offset by heavy operational losses attributed both to poor weather and aircrew inexperience.

This unusual photograph shows an anonymous F4F-3 taxiing into a hidden dispersal somewhere in the Pacific in early 1942. Judging by the vegetation, this shot may have been taken on one of the Hawaiian islands, although exactly where and when remains a mystery. Carved out of the undergrowth, the dirt taxyways lead to individual one-aircraft revetments. The Wildcat in the distance has had camouflage netting hung over it to further hide its position from the air *(via Aeroplane)*

This February 1942 action shot shows a VF-3 F4F-3 being given the signal to launch by the deck officer, who is gesturing with his arms outstretched in the foreground. All this is taking place aboard USS *Lexington*, which was steaming 400 miles off Rabaul, New Britain, at the time. 'Fighting Three', capably led by Lt Cdr John S Thach, were about to make naval history by repelling a formation of 17 Mitsubishi G4M 'Betty' bombers sent to sink their temporary home. Two months after this action, 'Lex' lost both her weighty, but near useless, eight in turrets (seen here in the background) during a quick refit, and received 1.1 in quad anti-aircraft guns in their place *(via Aeroplane)*

The next operation was also aborted, but, ironically, it produced naval aviation's first hero of the war. *Lexington* was detected by Japanese recce aircraft some 400 miles off Rabaul, New Britain, on 20 February and prepared to 'repel boarders'. A force of 17 Mitsubishi G4M 'Betty' bombers attacked, and were intercepted by Lt Cdr Thach's unit. VF-3's carrier, *Saratoga*, had received torpedo damage and was laid up for repairs, so it had replaced 'Lex's' VF-2, which was converting to F4Fs.

In a drawn-out action that afternoon, 'Fighting Three' splashed all but two of the raiders in exchange for one pilot and two Wildcats. Lt(jg) E H O'Hare found himself positioned to intercept with a wingman whose guns malfunctioned, but he dived in nonetheless. In three gunnery passes he expertly shot three bombers into the sea, mortally damaged another which crashed on its return flight to base, and set another on fire. Credited with five victories in his first combat, he was hailed as the Navy's first ace of the war. Awarded the Medal of Honor, he was immediately promoted two ranks to lieutenant commander and became a unit CO. He would return to combat flying F6F-3 Hellcats in late 1943, and eventually perish soon after in circumstances still not clear to this day.

There followed more *Enterprise* raids on Wake (24 February) and Marcus Islands (4 March), capped by a joint *Lexington-Yorktown* operation against Lae, New Guinea, on 10 March. Japanese shipping was sunk and damaged, and aerial resistance was marginal. However, the next operation in the same area would provoke an historic clash.

In early May Task Force 17 (*Lexington* and *Yorktown*) entered the Coral Sea, which washed the shores of Australia to the southwest and New Guinea to the northwest. The object was Japanese bases in the Solomon Islands, followed by the interception of an enemy troop convoy bound for Port Moresby, New Guinea. Thus was set into motion the first aircraft carrier duel in history.

On the 4th, Yorktown Air Group struck the naval air base at Tulagi, north of Guadalcanal. Some 14 ships were claimed sunk (actually three were destroyed) against meagre aerial opposition. A VF-42 section heard calls for help from VT-5 and engaged a trio of Mitsubishi F1M 'Pete' floatplanes, claiming all three.

The two-day Battle of the Coral Sea began on 7 May, and Task Force 17 had things all its own way. Despite confused scouting reports, a 93-plane strike group from both US carriers found the Japanese covering group built around the light carrier *Shoho*. In a set-piece attack reminiscent of a prewar drill, the carrier was smothered under a rain of bombs and torpedoes as her fighters tried to defend her. The Japanese launched a futile mixture of A5Ms and A6M2s – the first combat between Zeros and Navy F4Fs. The 'Yorktowners' had the best of it, VF-42's Lt Cdr James H Flatley splashing an A5M while Ens Walter A Haas bagged the first A6M kill by a Navy Wildcat pilot. He then added an A5M as well. The F4Fs got away clean, with VF-2 adding a floatplane en route to the target.

However, that same afternoon the Americans came under attack. The enemy covering force, composed of Pearl Harbor veterans *Shokaku* and *Zuikaku*, launched 27 aircraft which went after TF-17 as dusk settled. Thirty F4Fs hunted through the gloom, aided by ship-based radar controllers who gave VF-2's Lt Cdr Paul Ramsey initial contact. The two units destroyed or damaged 11 raiders, losing a Wildcat and a pilot each.

Described as naval aviation's first hero of the war (he was also its first ace), Lt(jg) Edward 'Butch' O'Hare made headline news following his quick-fire destruction of five 'Betty' bombers out of the 17 sent to attack *Lexington* on 20 February 1942. He only made three passes at the formation, but his aim was well up to the mark, and he was duly awarded the Medal of Honor soon after his return to the carrier

'Butch' O'Hare is congratulated by his skipper, Lt Cdr 'Jimmy' Thach (right). Taken well after the former's Medal of Honor mission off Rabaul, New Britain, this photo was one of many circulated by the Navy at the time. Thach and O'Hare were widely recognised as two of the finest aerial gunners in the Navy before the war, and both men proved their reputations in combat. Thach later became a F4F ace in the Battle of Midway, running his tally to six victories (*via Robert L Lawson*)

The battle continued the next day as both forces exchanged air strikes. Again *Lexington* and *Yorktown* units strove for a co-ordinated attack, but weather favoured the Japanese, whose carriers steamed under lowering clouds. VF-42 flew close escort on VT-5, keeping up their airspeed by weaving above the sluggish TBDs. Though intercepted by Zeros, *Yorktown's* F4Fs did a good job, fighting at a disadvantage but allowing all the Devestators to escape. Two SBDs were lost, however.

Lexington Air Group did not fare as well. Widely dispersed in clouds, tactical cohesion also suffered from the low airspeed flown by the escort leader. With Lt Noel Gayler's F4Fs deprived of any initiative, Zeros shot down three in exchange for one A6M, while the air group commander and another SBD crew were lost. Though *Shokaku* took bomb damage, she survived the day. *Lexington* would not.

Sixty-nine Japanese aircraft found TF-17 under clear skies, opposed by 17 Wildcats and 23 Dauntlesses on low-level anti-torpedo-plane patrol. The F4Fs, fighting by sections and divisions, engaged in a series of interceptions covering miles of ocean and thousands of feet in altitude. Despite optimistic Japanese claims, the F4Fs suffered four losses while the outclassed SBDs lost five. However, US aviators and shipboard gunners accounted for 19 attackers, and probably saved *Yorktown* from additional bomb hits. But *Lexington* was mortally wounded by aerial torpedoes and sank that evening, taking 33 aircraft to the bottom of the Coral Sea.

Both sides learned much from this first battle, especially the fighter units. The F4F's performance disparity with the A6M came as a surprise – the latter was faster, climbed better and turned tighter. Lessons had to be learnt quickly as an even greater battle was just 30 days away.

One of the most famous of all F4F photos was taken in Hawaiian waters on 10 April 1942. Flying 'Fox One' is John S Thach, while 'Butch' O'Hare flies formation in F-13. Thach's aircraft bears three rising-sun victory flags and O'Hare's five. On 20 February, when he was credited with downing five 'Bettys', O'Hare flew BuNo 4031, side number F-15 *(via Robert L Lawson)*

VF-42 pilots aboard *Yorktown*, 6 February 1942. Front, left to right: B T Macomber, A J Brassfield, R M Plott, W N Leonard, C F Fenton (XO), O Pederson (CO), V F McCormack, W S Woolen, L L Knox. Rear: E D Mattson, R L Wright, H B Gibbs, W W Barnes, J D Baker, E S McCuskey, R G Crommelin, J P Adams, W A Haas. Before Coral Sea, Pederson was 'fleeted up' to air group commander and was succeeded by Fenton as CO *(via Robert L Lawson)*

MIDWAY

The last week in May was a frenetic period for the Pacific Fleet fighting squadrons. Not only were they still absorbing the latest Wildcat model, but they had to prepare for a hasty departure from Pearl Harbor. It was hard enough for *Enterprise's* VF-6 and *Hornet's* untried VF-8 to get to grips with their myriad problems, but *Yorktown's* entire air group had the further strain of a total structural reorganisation while 'Old Yorky' entered dry dock for repairs to her battle damage.

Owing to heavy losses at Coral Sea, most of *Yorktown's* prewar air group was put ashore, replaced by *Saratoga* squadrons. Lt Cdr Thach came aboard with a cadre from VF-3, but the majority of fighter pilots remained from VF-42. They had minimum time to both 'shake out' as a new unit, and learn their new aircraft.

The F4F-4 differed in two respects from the 'dash three': it possessed folding wings, allowing fighter strength to increase to 27 Wildcats per carrier, and its armament was raised from four guns to six. With no increase in power, the new Grumman was slower than its predecessor, with less ammunition. The increase in armament was attributed to a request by the Royal Navy, who wanted greater firepower in the Martlet to allow it to cope with its German and Italian foes. US fighter pilots, accustomed to dealing with less well-armed Japanese aircraft, were not pleased.

Jimmy Thach spoke for most naval aviators when he said, 'A pilot who cannot hit with four guns will miss with eight'. Therefore, he relied on superior tactics to equalise the Zero's better performance. In the few days available, he trained the squadron in his 'beam defense' method of mutual support. It would shortly become famous as the 'Thach Weave'.

Behind the scenes at CinCPacFleet, one of the most significant intelligence intercepts of the war was being evaluated – American cryptanalysts had detected Adm Isoruko Yamamoto's plan for the capture of Midway Atoll, 1100 miles northwest of Oahu. Thus, Rear Adm Raymond Spruance departed with *Enterprise* and *Hornet* in Task Force 16, while Rear Adm Frank Jack Fletcher remained aboard *Yorktown* with Task Force 17. Three US carriers were committed against four of Vice Adm Chuichi Nagumo's veteran flattops. The greatest battle of the Pacific War to date would determine the fate of Hawaii.

Midway itself was jam packed with Army, Navy and Marine Corps aircraft, including VMF-221. Primarily equipped with the Brewster F2A-3 Buffalo, Maj Floyd Parks' squadron also possessed seven ex-Navy F4F-3s.

'Fighting Six' Wildcats with SBD-3 Dauntlesses ranged on *Enterprise's* flight deck in May 1942. The obvious marking difference from the immediate post-Pearl Harbor period is the return of the national insignia to six positions (top and bottom of both wings), but without the red 'meatball' centre. VF-6 entered the Battle of Midway in June with 27 F4F-4s, the first combat for the six-gun, folding-wing, variant of the Grumman fighter. Naval aviators were widely disappointed in the new version, which proved both heavier and slower, and was equipped with less ammunition than the F4F-3 *(via Robert L Lawson)*

The Wildcats were assigned to the squadron's fifth division under Capt John F Carey, as some of his pilots had at least prevuiously flown the type in San Diego. However, there was precious little time to sort out the newly-arrived Grummans before Nagumo launched his first strike at dawn on 4 June.

Alerted by radar, Midway scrambled 25 fighters barely in time to intercept 107 enemy carrier bombers and fighters. In a lopsided 15-minute battle, VMF-221 was cut to pieces, with 15 fighters being lost, including two F4Fs – the Wildcats had got off easier than they might have. Carey's fifth division was denied the chance to fight as a unit, owing to confusion generated by the inbound air raid. Up on CAP at dawn, six of the seven F4Fs patrolled until ordered to land, though two Wildcats did not hear the recall. When the scramble came, another F4F became bogged down in the sand and could not take-off with Carey. Though all six operational F4Fs did engage the enemy, they attacked piecemeal.

The Marine pilots were credited with 10 shootdowns (five by the Wildcats), which seemed to track with the 10 Japanese combat losses. However, Midway's AA gunners apparently did most of the damage, and historian John B Lundstrom has since determined that the fighters got three kills at most. Regardless of the actual score, VMF-221 was now effectively out of the battle.

Northeast of Midway, the two US task forces awaited word of Nagumo's appearance. Once his presence was confirmed, Spruance and Fletcher independently launched deckload strikes from each carrier. However, the F4F's contribution to this phase of the battle was severely limited both by circumstance and fate.

Having seen the capabilities of Japanese air groups a month before, Vice Adm Fletcher's staff retained most of *Yorktown's* fighters for task-force defense. Thach, and five of his pilots, flew close escort to VT-3, while Bombing Three climbed to altitude, hunting Nagumo. The F4Fs were stretching their fuel and their luck almost to breaking point – Thach, for instance, offered to push the escort out to 175 miles.

Meanwhile, *Enterprise* and *Hornet* launched larger escorts for their respective bombers and 'torpeckers', but to little avail. Lt J S Gray, skipper of VF-6, unknowingly tacked onto *Hornet's* TBDs. Unable to communicate with Torpedo Eight, he remained overhead with ten Wildcats, reporting to *Enterprise*, while VT-8 attacked the enemy carriers unescorted and was destroyed. Soon after, VT-6 also

VMF-221 entered the Battle of Midway with 20 Brewster F2A Buffaloes and seven Wildcats. However, the unit sustained severe losses during the morning of 4 June, with 15 pilots killed and several more wounded. This F4F-3 was shot up by Zeros and barely made it back to Midway, where it was crash-landed by wounded pilot, Capt John F Carey. Ironically, despite the F2A's miserable reputation after Midway, many pilots preferred the Buffalo to the F4F due to it being more responsive, although it was a less stable gun platform *(via Robert L Lawson)*

VF-6's 'Fox Seven' takes off from *Enterprise* on 18 May 1942, shortly before the carrier sailed for Midway. One variation on standard markings is the black numeral 'seven' well forward on the fuselage, minus the usual F prefix. Commanded by Lt James S Gray during the battle, VF-6 claimed nine aircraft shot down and two damaged. Only one of 'The Big E's' F4Fs was lost in return – a water landing with the pilot recovered *(via Robert L Lawson)*

went in alone and suffered severe losses. At the same time VF-8's ten Grummans were lost when their CO ran them out of fuel while trying to remain with the longer-ranged SBDs. Two pilots died in water landings.

Only the 'Yorktowners' reached the target intact, Thach's six F4Fs fighting a desperate battle against the odds in order to protect VT-3 from the Japanese interceptors. In the first combat test of the 'Thach Weave', the VF-3 pilots constantly brought guns to bear on Zeros dogging one anothers' tails. Thus negating the opposition's superior performance, the Wildcats tied up part of the Japanese CAP while claiming five kills and two probables for one loss. But the 130-knot TBDs had little chance, and none returned to *Yorktown*.

However, as Thach turned away he witnessed a miracle in the making. Three Japanese carriers were burning themselves to destruction, victims of three SBD squadrons which arrived unhindered at high altitude. Making superb use of a priceless five minutes, the *Enterprise* and *Yorktown* scout-bombers destroyed HIMJS *Akagi*, *Kaga* and *Soryu*. The battle had completely reversed.

But *Hiryu* remained afloat, with a largely-intact air group. Thanks to reconnaissance by cruiser-based floatplanes, the location of TF-17 was now known to the Japanese, who immediately launched 18 Aichi D3A 'Val' dive bombers, escorted by four Zeros. They were met by a dozen VF-3 Wildcats, which benefited from accurate radar information and a little help from TF-16 fighters. In a frantic few minutes 11 'Vals' went down, including three each credited to Lt(jg)s E S McCuskey and A J Brassfield of VF-3. *Yorktown's* gunners splashed another bomber, but the remainder got through, hitting CV-5 three times. Listing badly, she lost steerageway and went dead in the water.

Hiryu was already preparing another strike: ten Nakajima B5N 'Kate'

Seven F4F-4s of *Hornet's* VF-8 during the Battle of Midway. Individual aircraft numbers appear on the fuselage and in large, non-standard positions high on the engine cowlings. Like most of Hornet Air Group, 'Fighting Eight' put in a disappointing performance during the crucial engagement, claiming just five victories in exchange for 12 aircraft and three pilots lost to all causes. Thus, VF-8 inflicted the least damage on the Japanese while sustaining the highest losses of the three carrier fighter squadrons engaged *(via Robert L Lawson)*

The top-scoring fighter pilot in the Battle of Midway was VF-3's Lt(jg) E Scott McCuskey, a VF-42 veteran. On 4 June 'Doc' McCuskey flew two intercepts, claiming three 'Val' dive bombers and two Zero fighters in defense of *Yorktown*. He thus became the top Navy ace of the first six months of the Pacific War with 6.50 victories. He later added eight more kills flying F6F Hellcats with the new VF-8 from the Essex-class carrier *Bunker Hill* in 1944 (*via Robert L Lawson*)

torpedo planes with six escorts. Zeros were scarce by then, as three had been shot down over *Yorktown*.

The US carriers had also respotted their decks, reinforcing the CAP. Airborne VF-3 pilots recovered aboard *Enterprise*, refuelled and rearmed, and were ready when the second enemy attack arrived. Superb damage control had got *Yorktown* back up to 19 knots in less than three hours, allowing the resumption of air operations. However, some of Thach's pilots were still cranking up their wheels when the 'Kates' descended in high-speed approaches. At a cost of two F4Fs lost to Zeros, VF-3 splashed five 'Kates' and two Zeros, with McCuskey running his one-day total to five. But tragically VF-8's misfortune continued as a *Hornet* pilot was killed by 'friendly' AA fire as well.

Despite a spirited defense, some of the Nakajimas penetrated the CAP and shipboard flak to put two torpedoes into *Yorktown*. It was too much for the carrier to withstand, and Capt Buckmaster ordered 'abandon ship'. Therefore, Vice Adm Fletcher, the senior officer afloat, was effectively out of the battle. He turned over conduct of the battle to Rear Adm Raymond Spruance in TF-16.

Late that afternoon SBDs from *Enterprise* and *Yorktown* found the remains of the Japanese force and quickly sunk *Hiryu*. However, owing to the uncertainty about other enemy carriers in the area, all available F4Fs were retained for CAP. The Wildcat's role in the crucial Battle of Midway was essentially over. When *Yorktown* succumbed to a Japanese submarine at dawn on 7 June 1942, the naval engagement was finally over.

Three new aces were crowned at Midway – Thach (6), McCuskey (6.5) and Brassfield (6.33), joining O'Hare and Lt N A Gayler (5 each). Additionally, VF-3/-42 produced Lt(jg)s W A Haas with 4.83 victories and W N Leonard with four. Therefore, after six months of war the top seven fighter pilots in the US Navy had flown wholly or partly with 'Fighting Three'. During the same period, the five carrier fighter squadrons had claimed 113.5 victories, split the following way:

VF-3	Lexington, Yorktown	50.5
VF-42	Yorktown	25
VF-2	Lexington	17
VF-6	Enterprise	16
VF-8	Hornet	5

Sadly, when VF-42 was disestablished after Midway, the Navy's most experienced fighter squadron passed into history. However, by this stage the Mitsubishi Zero had been proven beatable. At the end of this first phase of the war, the F4F's exchange rate against the A6M stood at 1.5 to 1. It would remain the high figure for the rest of the year.

GUADALCANAL

Despite the institutional experience gained at Coral Sea and Midway, some F4F squadrons still knew little about the opposition. For example, Lt L H Bauer, the new CO of *Enterprise*'s VF-6, later stated that the Zero was an unknown quantity to most of his pilots. In fact, after initial combat in the Solomons, 'Fighting Six' considered removing the outboard machine gun in each wing in order to 'lighten ship' and improve manoeuvrability. This ignorance of the enemy's capabilities saw the carrier fighters begin the first American offensive of the war totally ill-prepared – they paid a high price in men and machines as a result.

Operation *Watchtower* began at dawn on 7 August 1942. Supporting the invasion of Guadalcanal were three PacFleet carriers: *Saratoga, Enterprise* and *Wasp*. They entered combat with 98 fighters, as the nominal complement now was 36 per squadron. *Wasp* had no combat experience, but she had twice delivered RAF Spitfires to Malta earlier in the year, and her air group was night qualified – a rare advantage at the time.

The Japanese command at Rabaul, New Britain, launched 27 'Bettys' and 17 Zeros, plus nine 'Vals' which were to be sacrificed beyond their tactical radius. Of the 18 Wildcats that intercepted from VF-5 and -6, no less than nine were shot down. Five 'Bettys' and two A6Ms went down, plus all the 'Vals', the latter either from combat or fuel exhaustion. Beyond that, however, the VF squadrons lost another six aircraft to various causes, and, in total, six pilots – it remained the F4F's worst ever one-day loss to enemy aircraft. A *Wasp* SBD was also shot down.

In retrospect, the interceptions started poorly and disintegrated rapidly. Too few F4Fs were airborne at the outset – one division was misdirected away from the battle, and others were caught at a tactical disadvantage. Attacked from above, they were defeated in detail. Beyond that, the Americans faced high-quality opponents. The Tainan Air Group boasted most of Japan's top fighter aces at the time – veterans like Petty Officers Saburo Sakai and Horiyoshi Nishizawa, both with many victories to their credit. The fact that the Zero pilots optimistically claimed some 40 kills did nothing to reduce their impact on the American aviators.

Among the most successful F4F pilots during the landings was a warrant officer – Machinist Donald E Runyon of VF-6. Formerly a NAP, the soft-spoken Runyon was widely regarded as one of the finest fighter pilots in the US Navy. He lived up to his reputation with credits for two

The Navy's top F4F ace was Machinist Donald E Runyon, formerly an enlisted pilot, who scored eight aerial victories in three combats during August 1942. On the 7th, the day of the initial Guadalcanal landings, the VF-6 flier claimed two Aichi D3A dive bombers, followed the next day by a Mitsubishi bomber and a Zero. On the 24th, during the Battle of the Eastern Solomons, he destroyed three more Aichis and a Zero. Later commissioned, Runyon returned to combat in 1943-44 and added three more victories flying F6Fs with VF-18 from *Bunker Hill* *(via Robert L Lawson)*

bombers on the 7th and a 'Betty' and a Zero on the 8th. He would shortly become the Navy's leading F4F ace, a distinction he would retain for the remainder of the war.

When Vice Adm Fletcher withdrew his three carriers from the landing area, the Marines ashore were left without air cover. To make matters worse, a strong Japanese surface force pummelled Allied warships that night in the lopsided Battle of Savo Island. Bereft of all support, the transports departed with most of their cargo still aboard. Thus, the 1st Marine Division was left entirely on its own. However, two squadrons were quickly dispatched aboard the escort carrier *Long Island* (CVE-1), which reached a launch position on 20 August. Nineteen Wildcats and a dozen Dauntlesses of VMF-223 and VMSB-232 respectively, landed at Henderson Field, Guadalcanal, that evening. They became the original 'plankowners' of the 'Cactus Air Force'.

Newly-promoted Maj John L Smith had no combat, and little leadership, experience, but he built a winning team in VMF-223. Over the next few days he, and his largely-untried lieutenants, took the measure of their opponents. Smith and his engineering officer, Capt Marion E Carl (a Midway survivor), would become the first major American aces of World War 2. Combined with Lt Col Richard C Mangrum's scout-bombers, they soon began making their presence felt among Japanese units in the Solomon Islands.

The war's third aircraft carrier duel occurred on 24 August, but the land-based Marines also had a role to play. Supported by part of an Army Air Force P-39/P-400 squadron, Smith's pilots fought their first major engagement that afternoon. They intercepted six 'Kate' level bombers, escorted by 15 Zeros, off HIMJS *Ryujo* and, in a frantic, confusing, tussle, shot down seven raiders for the loss of three Wildcats and two pilots. It was an important victory, proving that Marine fighters could more than hold their own. Additionally, in this combat Marion Carl became the first fighter ace of the US Marine Corps – a further 120 others would follow in his slipstream over the next three years.

At sea, Fletcher had detached *Wasp* for refuelling, but retained *Enterprise* and *Saratoga* to meet the first Japanese attempt to reinforce Guadalcanal. The battle turned upon communications, which, if anything favoured Vice Adm Nagumo's force with Coral Sea veterans *Shokaku* and *Zuikaku*. Poor-quality radios conspired with atmospheric conditions to allow an unescorted *Saratoga* strike to sink *Ryujo*, but to miss the greater threat.

Meanwhile, the two Japanese air groups had little difficulty finding their target. Late that afternoon 27 'Vals' and ten Zeros attacked 'The Big E,' fighting their way through no fewer than 53 airborne Wildcats of VF-5 and -6. Initial radar contact was made at some 90 miles – an excellent performance for the equipment – so the Americans had adequate warning. In the race to meet the incoming raid, one division of VF-5 made a record 'pit

Maj John L Smith led VMF-223, the first fighter squadron ashore on Guadalcanal. From 20 August to 16 October, he was credited with 19 kills, while his unit claimed a total of 110. Upon returning to America, Smith was awarded the Medal of Honor as the nation's then top ace. At war's end he remained the second-ranked Wildcat pilot behind Maj Joe Foss. Tough, aggressive and wholly mission-oriented, Smith was regarded as one of the premier unit commanders ever produced by the 'Corps *(via Robert L Lawson)*

Reportedly a VMF-223 aircraft, this F4F-4 remains something of a mystery. It has been described as one of John L Smith's Wildcats, but the significance of the 19 victory flags remains unknown. Even more questionable is the odd rendering of the numeral two, which appears to have been modified from another figure. The early Wildcat squadrons at 'Cactus' usually assigned specific aircraft to individual pilots, but the practise eventually broke down as maintenance and losses dictated otherwise *(via Robert L Lawson)*

stop', refuelling and taking off again in just 11 minutes.

But the situation was compounded early on, largely owing to communications problems. In 1942 the US Navy still lacked enough radio frequencies to handle search, strike and fighter direction tasks independently of one another. Consequently, available channels became crowded, and vital information never reached airborne pilots.

Morever, not all the F4Fs were able to engage, and despite heavy losses, the Japanese aviators exhibited a high degree of professionalism. They hit *Enterprise* three times, inflicting serious damage, and forcing many of her aircraft to recover aboard 'Sara', or to land ashore. Incredibly, a follow-up Japanese strike group came within 50 miles of the US task force and might have finished 'The Big E' off, but inexplicably turned back instead.

The Wildcat pilots submitted claims of 45 'bandits' splashed, while the SBDs and TBFs claimed eight more. Although the actual Japanese losses were nowwhere near as dramatic (Nagumo only launched 37 aircraft in total!), the Americans actually shot down, or mortally damaged, 25 machines – two-thirds of those launched against Fletcher. *Zuikaku's* entire nine-plane bomber squadron was lost on this mission.

One of the American aviators responsible for the Japanese losses was Donald Runyon, the VF-6 pilot being credited with four victories on 7-8 August. He matched that total again on the 24th, claiming three 'Vals' and a Zero for a total of eight credited victories in just three combats during the month. No carrier pilot would surpass his record for a year-and-a-half. Like many veterans of the 1942 battles, Runyon returned to combat in 1944, adding three more victories to his logbook while flying Hellcats.

The Battle of the Eastern Solomons confirmed many of the lessons first learned at Coral Sea and Midway. The crucial importance of scouting and communications was reinforced, but carrier fighter doctrine had largely matured to its full potential with the F4F. Fighter direction continued improving throughout the year as well, ultimately evolving into the superb system in place by 1944. Additionally, *Enterprise* and *Saratoga* demonstrated flexibility in operating one anothers' Wildcats smoothly and efficiently.

Fighter operations ashore were also functioning with greater efficiency. Thanks to the coastwatchers – Australian or British military and political officers, planters and missionaries – advance warning of Japanese air raids gave land-based Wildcats the 45 minutes they needed to get to altitude. However, the coastwatcher network was hampered in poor weather, when high-flying aircraft could not be seen. The situation improved somewhat in early September with arrival of the Third Defense Battalion's radar set at Henderson Field. This combination of human and electronic early warning was crucial to intercepting inbound raids. And there was seldom a shortage of enemy aircraft: in the three weeks beginning 21

Perhaps the most distinctive form of victory markings applied to Wildcats were VF-6's 'tombstones', which appeared towards the end of their eventful Pacific deployment in September 1942. Each F4F-4 aboard *Enterprise* sported the emblem, with 41 Japanese suns representing the squadron's claims from the Guadalcanal campaign – in truth, records reveal 43 victories from 7 to 24 August. Rather appropriately, the pilot who contributed more than his fair share to this tally, Machinist Donald Runyon, is seen here posing alongside the marking applied to his Wildcat. Three other aces spent time with VF-6 at some point or another during this historic cruise – Lt(jg) F R Register (6.50 kills, also flew with VF-5), AP1/c L P Mankin (5 kills, and also spent time with VF-5) and Lt A O Vorse, Jr, (5 kills, and flew with VF-2 and -3) *(via Robert L Lawson)*

August Japanese land- and carrier-based squadrons attacked the US beach-head ten times, averaging more than 30 aircraft per raid.

With repeated opportunities, Smith and his engineering officer, Capt Marion Carl, quickly became the first triple aces of the US armed forces in World War 2. Despite VMF-223 being reinforced by Maj Robert E Galer's VMF-224 on 30 August, the F4Fs were nearly always outnumbered, even with the addition of the Bell P-39 *Airacobras* of the USAAF's 67th Fighter Squadron. However, the lopsided odds ensured frequent combat for the Marines. For instance, on 26 August Carl was jumped in the landing pattern, cranked up his wheels and engaged the audacious Zero over the beach – his quarry exploded before hundreds of witnesses. His victim was quite possibly Lt Junichi Sasai, a well-regarded leader of the Tainan Kokutai, who had claimed four victories on 7 August alone.

Despite near-constant combat, improvements were steadily made at 'Cactus'. One of the most important was begun in late August when a grassy expanse east of Henderson Field was prepared for operation. Officially designated the 'Fighter Strip' (and later 'Fighter One'), it was commonly called the 'cow pasture' due to its rural nature. Aside from relieving some of the congestion at Henderson, it allowed Wildcat squadrons to operate more independently.

During this same period, 'Cactus' became the unexpected recipient of yet another fighter squadron. On 31 August – a week after the Eastern Solomons carrier duel – *Saratoga* was torpedoed by a Japanese submarine for the second time in eight months. The damage was not severe, but most of the air group went ashore while the big flat-top received repairs. Consequently, Lt Cdr Leroy Simpler's VF-5 rounded out a three-service contingent to 'Cactus Fighter Command'. On 11 September 'Fighting Five' arrived with 24 Wildcats. Five weeks later only four of those aircraft remained. The unit's aces were Mark K Bright, Hayden M Jensen, Carlton B Starkes and John M Wesolowski, who scored their kills whilst mostly flying from Guadalcanal. The Navy's only enlisted ace also emerged from the campaign – Aviation Pilot 1st Class Lee P Mankin, who flew with VF-5 from *Saratoga* and VF-6 from *Enterprise*.

Marine aviators also were also scoring heavily at the same time – VMF-224's CO, Maj Bob Galer, ran his tally into double figures, as did Lt Col Harold 'Indian Joe' Bauer of VMF-212. Bauer, possibly the finest fighter pilot in the Marine Corps, managed several 'guest appearance' missions with -223 prior to his own squadron arriving at Guadalcanal in force. It was an ironic situation, as Carl and Bauer had first encountered one another while flying F3Fs in VMF-1 three years before. A rivalry had soon developed between the two, but was resolved when, in VMF-221 at San Diego in 1941, they had squared off in Brewster F2As and, in Carl's words, 'went at it man to man'. The mock dogfight ended in a draw, with neither pilot gaining an advantage. From that beginning a warm, respectful, friendship emerged.

Bauer's best day came on 3 October when, leading a division in Marion Carl's flight, 'the coach' claimed four Zeros confirmed, with another probably destroyed. Carl, who scored one victory in the same combat, was almost as pleased with his friend's success as Bauer himself.

The next fighter reinforcement took the form of Maj Leonard K 'Duke' Davis' VMF-121, which arrived on 9 October. Launched from the escort carrier *Copahee* (CVE-12), the fresh squadron added 24 much-needed F4Fs to the 'Cactus Air Force'. Davis's executive officer was to become the leading ace not only of the campaign, but of the Marine Corps. Capt Joseph J Foss had connived his way out of a photo squadron into fighters, and immediately began setting records. He claimed his first victory just four days after landing on Guadalcanal, and became an ace five days after that! On 25 October he became the Marines' first ace in a day, credited with five Zeros in two missions.

However, by early October VMF-223 and -224 were largely a spent force, the unrelenting pace of operations resulting in their removal from the theatre, despite there being few replacements to 'step into the breech'. On 12 October Smith left 'The Canal' with 19 victories, and Carl was close behind with 16.5. Four days later Joe Bauer again made his presence felt. USS *McFarland*, an old destroyer that had been converted into a fast transport, arrived at 'Cactus' with much-needed aviation fuel and ordnance. As gasoline was being barged ashore, nine 'Val' dive bombers evaded the F4F CAP, arrived overhead, and immediately attacked. One enemy pilot bombed the barge, which exploded in a geyser of flame – the explosion also inflicted fatal damage on *McFarland*.

At that moment, Bauer was leading VMF-212 into the 'Fighter Strip' following a long ferry flight from Espiritu Santo. Low on fuel, but with full ammunition, 'The Coach' again showed his team how 'the game was played'. He dived into the 'Vals', and working his way from back to front, flamed three in succession. Only a shortage of fuel prevented him from splashing more.

SANTA CRUZ

The Santa Cruz Islands, which lent their name to the fourth aircraft carrier battle, had no geographic impact upon the Guadalcanal campaign. Lying some 300 miles east of the Solomons, they were so remote from 'Cactus' that they might as well have never pushed up from the ocean floor as far as the hard-pressed USMC pilots were concerned. However, the fleet engagement of 26 October 1942 *was* an integral part of the see-saw contest for control of Henderson Field. The naval-air duel off Santa Cruz was intended by the Japanese to cover a major reinforcement attempt of Guadalcanal. Several postponements by the Japanese 17th Army delayed the overall effort until 25 October. Thus, the stage was set for a new Wildcat squadron's debut in the war's largest theatre.

'Fighting Ten' was part of Air Group Ten, the first such organization committed to combat under a numerical designation instead of a ship's name. However, its home – the *Enterprise*, patched up from her Eastern Solomons damage of late August – was far from new to combat . The skipper of VF-10 was Lt Cdr J H Flatley, who had fought Zeros as a *Yorktown* pilot at Coral Sea. His 'Grim Reapers' boasted 34 Wildcats going into the battle, which finally commenced following preliminary manoeuvring and a false alarm air strike on the evening of the 25th.

Enterprise was teamed with *Hornet*, still flying a hodge-podge air group which included only two of her own squadrons. Her fighter strength comprised 38 F4Fs of VF-72, led by Lt Cdr H G Sanchez. Though both carriers operated independently, overall command rested with Rear Adm T C Kinkaid, riding in 'The Big E'.

Widely acknowledged as one of the finest aviators of all time, Marion E Carl first gained attention as a fighter pilot. Flying with VMF-221 at Midway and -223 at Guadalcanal, he claimed 16.5 victories in F4Fs and finished as the third-ranking Wildcat ace. He led -223 on its second combat tour, adding two more kills in F4U-1 Corsairs during 1943-44. Following the war, as a lieutenant colonel, Carl established world altitude and speed records, conducted early jet tests aboard carriers, and pioneered Marine Corps helicopters. While a flag officer he flew jet and helicopter missions in Vietnam, retiring as a major general in 1973 *(via Robert L Lawson)*

Opposing Task Force 61 were four Japanese carriers, again led by Vice Adm Chuichi Nagumo. Santa Cruz would mark his final appearance as a carrier leader; like Kinkaid, he was not an aviator. However, Nagumo was vastly more experienced.

The Santa Cruz odds of four carriers to two represented the greatest disparity that American carrier men would face during the war. The highly-experienced *Shokaku* and *Zuikaku* were joined by the CVLs *Zuiho* and *Junyo*, with the latter operating in the advance force. Nagumo's Zero *hikotais* thus outnumbered the US Navy fighter force, the former boasting 82 Zeros compared with 72 F4F-4s. Unlike the recent Eastern Solomons battle, no land-based fighters were involved, even peripherally.

Each force knew the other's location and launched air strikes almost simultaneously. The Japanese were first off the mark with a co-ordinated 64-machine strike from *Shokaku*, *Zuikaku* and *Zuiho*. *Hornet's* first launch included two VF-72 divisions escorting 15 scout-bombers and six torpedo aircraft. A half-hour behind was a smaller *Enterprise* contingent: 11 strike aircraft screened by eight VF-10 Wildcats. About the same time *Hornet's* final contribution departed the task force, again with two VF-72 divisions (short one F4F for a total of seven) escorting 18 bombers.

Still climbing outbound, the Air Group 10 formation was caught low and slow barely 60 miles from TF-61. Nine *Junyo* Zeros, escorting their own strike aircraft, could not resist the temptation. They initiated a surprise attack from above and behind the *Enterprise* group, and played merry hell. One Avenger fell immediately, with two more forced down with heavy damage. Lt John Leppla's division, responsible for protecting the TBFs, was shredded to pieces. Leppla, a *Lexington* Coral Sea veteran, was soon killed, while two of his wingmen were shot down and captured. The sole surviving pilot of the division nursed his battle-damaged fighter for more than three hours before returning to *Enterprise*.

The other F4F division was led by Lt Cdr Flatley, skipper of 'Fighting Ten'. Shrugging off the initial Zero avalanche, his pilots dropped their external tanks, turned into the threat and fought back. Flatley splashed a persistent Japanese fighter then regrouped.

The 'Grim Reapers' of VF-10 pose in front of their impressively decorated scoreboard alongside the island on *Enterprise* at the end of their first tour in February 1943. Entering combat in October 1942, 'The Big E' squadron was instrumental in the carrier battle of Santa Cruz and the later defense of Guadalcanal. Under the gifted leadership of Lt Cdr James H Flatley (front, fifth from left), the first-tour 'Reapers' claimed 43 shootdowns and eventually produced ten aces. One of the few carrier fighter squadrons with three combat tours, VF-10 logged cruises in F6F Hellcats during 1944, again in 'The Big E', and F4U Corsairs from *Intrepid* in 1945
(via Robert L Lawson)

This confused shootout resulted in five US losses against four Zeros. A surviving TBF aborted with engine problems before the three remaining Avengers attacked a cruiser, without result. After a Dauntless trio independently near-missed another cruiser, the main *Enterprise* strike had exhausted its weapons, achieving little for their efforts. There was no option but to turn for home.

However, unknown to aviators on either side, two *Enterprise* SBDs had managed to ambush Nagumo by inflicting bomb damage on *Zuiho*. One-quarter of the Japanese flight decks were now out of commission.

Hornet's first strike then came across the same surface force that attracted the *Enterprise* survivors. Both the VB- and VS-8 aircrews had been deprived of a shot at enemy carriers at Midway, and they were determined to tackle the surviving flat-tops. Consequently, the SBDs flew on past the crippled *Zuiho* and pressed on northward, where they were rewarded with a chance of bombing *Shokaku*. VF-72 lost three F4Fs and pilots while protecting the dive bombers from the persistent Japanese CAP, but the Wildcats' sacrifice proved not to be in vain – *Hornet*'s Dauntlesses tipped into their 70-degree dives and hit *Shokaku* with three or more bombs, knocking her out of the battle. Additionally, the cruiser *Chikuma* had also been hit, and Sanchez's Wildcats, along with the SBD gunners, splashed at least five Zeros during the running gunfight. The odds against the Americans were rapidly diminishing.

Almost simultaneously 138 Japanese aircraft then began attacking Task Force 61. In addition to his initial strike of 64 aircraft, Nagumo had put up a second group composed of 19 dive bombers, 17 'Kates' and nine Zeros, as well as a third batch of 17 more 'Vals', with a dozen Zero escorts. These strikes would subject *Enterprise* and *Hornet* to the longest sustained air attack experienced by US carriers during the first two years of the war.

Though most of the Japanese squadrons were two hours flying time from TF-16, their staggered launch compressed the effect of their attacks. For almost three hours the US carriers were under actual, or impending, attack from five separate or co-ordinated formations which comprised 57 'Vals', 39 'Kates', 42 Zeros and three reconnaissance aircraft.

Zuikaku's 'Vals' preceded *Shokaku*'s 'Kates' in a 20-minute attack that started just before 0900. The 38 airborne Wildcats were too few to deal effectively with 40 attackers, let alone their Zero escorts, and the problem was compounded by poor communications and weather. The first interception was made only 20 miles out when eight VF-72 pilots contacted the 'Vals'. However, the F4Fs were too low to do much good, and they lost three of their number in exchange for a trio of 'Vals'.

Meanwhile, seven 'Vals' got a shot at *Hornet*. Though three splashed, the others made three hits, badly damaging the year-old carrier. Then the torpedo planes arrived. Only one *Hornet* pilot got among the raiders long enough to make a difference. His name was Ens George L Wrenn.

Separated from his leader, Wrenn duelled briefly with the 'Vals' and Zeros, then came across the speedy Nakajima torpedo planes. Joined by two other F4Fs, he shot two 'Kates' into the water. Then, alone, he engaged another pair and claimed their destruction. Finally, low on fuel and ammunition near the task force, he shot the wing off another Nakajima. During the mission Wrenn had tangled with eight hostiles and claimed five, thus becoming *Hornet*'s only ace.

Between F4Fs and AA guns, half the 'Kate' assault had been broken up. However, 11 more split to starboard, closing on the damaged carrier. Zeros kept the few available F4Fs off the Nakajimas, which pressed on through the screen's thick flak, and although *Hornet*'s gunners 'splashed' five 'Kates', two got close enough to put torpedoes into her hull. The carrier rapidly lost power and, listing to starboard, stopped dead in the water.

Japanese pressure was unrelenting. Next on the scene were *Shokaku*'s dive bombers, which attacked at 1015. It seemed as if a month's production from the Aichi plant had arrived overhead TF-61 all at once as *Enterprise*'s pilots fought D3As from both Japanese large carriers. Noting the abundance of targets, some pilots switched off two or even four of their six guns in order to conserve ammunition. Other problems also arose as drop tanks refused to release, further hindering the F4F-4's performance by gravely restricting the aircraft's manoeuvrability.

VF-10's 'Red Seven' division was led by Lt S W Vejtasa, better known as 'Swede'. A former *Yorktown* SBD pilot, he had joined the 'Grim Reapers' at Flatley's invitation, and immediately went to work. Orbiting the task force, he latched onto a string of 'Vals' headed for *Hornet*. He quickly shot two into the water, while one of his wingmen took care of a third dive-bomber.

By then *Zuikaku*'s 'Kates' had arrived, and Vejtasa tied into them, too. Detaching his second section, he led his wingman to intercept 11 of the speedy torpedo planes as they descended onto *Enterprise*. Chasing the green-painted Nakajimas in and out of clouds was hard enough, without the added danger of having to dodge 'friendly' flak, but Vejtasa persisted. In the next several minutes he rode up close to five B5Ns and sent them burning into the choppy grey waves. Then, out of ammunition, he could only watch in frustration as 'The Big E' was struck by two bombs. The task force then managed to evade *Junyo*'s 'Vals' for 20 minutes in the forenoon hour, low clouds preventing the raiders from concentrating their attacks – most bombs fell amongst *Enterprise*, the battleship *South Dakota* (BB-57) and the light cruiser *San Juan* (CL-54). Between combat, battle damage and fuel loss, 11 of the 17 bombers failed to return to *Junyo*.

However, the prolonged attack had worked against *Hornet*'s returning strike escort. After a long flight out and back, which had seen them lose three of their eight F4Fs, VF-72 pilots now had to shoot their way back home, only to find their ship unable to recover them. Heavily engaged was the division of Lt John S Sutherland, which claimed five kills, including two by Sutherland himself. Whatever the actual results of the Wildcats' attacks, VF-72's third division certainly helped disrupt *Junyo*'s bombing strikes on TF-61.

The last of the Japanese strikes took the form of *Junyo*'s six 'Kates'. Their appearance forced the cruiser *Northampton* (CA-26) to part *Hornet*'s tow line, and her escorting destroyers promptly stood clear. The Japanese leader put his torpedo into the carrier's starboard beam, but was then killed in a barrage of AA fire, along with one of his other crews. But the damage was done. With a 14-degree list, *Hornet* was abandoned, to be finished off by Japanese destroyers patrolling in the area that night.

By the time the surviving fighter pilots got aboard *Enterprise*, it was obvious that the Japanese had won the battle. That evening anxious avia-

Lt Stanley W Vejtasa set a record for Wildcat pilots with seven victories during one mission. On 26 October 1942, during the Santa Cruz engagement, the VF-10 aviator claimed five 'Vals' and two 'Kates', possibly saving *Enterprise* from destruction. Originally a *Yorktown* SBD pilot and a Coral Sea veteran, Vejtasa had been recruited into fighters by Lt Cdr Flatley, then of VF-42. Vejtasa received a well-deserved Navy Cross for his flying and gunnery at Santa Cruz. The significance of the victory flags on this F4F, side number 79, is unknown *(via Robert L Lawson)*

tors speculated on the fate of missing squadron-mates. In combat, or on operations, VF-10 and -72 had lost a staggering total of 23 Wildcats and 14 pilots, two of whom were prisoners. Another 10 F4Fs sank with *Hornet*, raising total American losses to 80 aircraft.

In all, TF-61 claimed 115 shootdowns – 67 by the two air groups (56 by F4Fs) and 48 by shipboard gunners. In fact, only 67 Japanese aircraft were actually shot down, John B Lundstrom's analysis concluding that near the US task force, enemy losses were almost evenly divided between fighter action and AA fire. However, another 28 Japanese aircraft ditched, or crashed with battle damage, and four more were lost aboard *Shokaku* and *Zuikaku* – making a total of 99.

In overall fighter comparison, the F4F edged out the Zero 15 to 13, though the figure approached parity if post-combat attrition is counted. The extent of battle damage leading to aircraft losses can never be known precisely, but this rough comparison demonstrates that properly-flown Wildcats were holding their own against the opposition.

Although tactically a Japanese victory, the Battle of Santa Cruz proved futile in the long run. The tenuous American grasp on Guadalcanal remained unchanged, and *Hornet* was the last US carrier sunk by an attack from the air for two years. Furthermore, the Imperial Navy had lost 145 skilled aircrew, including 23 experienced leaders. They were never replaced in kind.

'CACTUS' CLIMAX

After the failure of Japan's late-October effort to seize Guadalcanal, American strength gradually increased. Among fighter squadrons, individual replacement pilots trickled in to fill the gaps within battle-weary frontline units like VMF-121 and -223. Meanwhile, Maj Paul J Fontana's newly-arrived VMF-112 observed Armistice Day by claiming three bombers and two Zeros. They added nine more the next day, as the last crisis loomed at Guadalcanal.

Overlooked in most histories of the 'Cactus Air Force' is the contribution of VMO-251. Ostensibly an observation squadron, Maj John Hart's unit flew F4F-4s, as well as the 'dash seven' photo-recce variants. On 11 November the squadron's pilots, on detached duty to 'Cactus', began shooting down enemy aircraft, the first two being a Zero and a bomber credited to Maj W R Campbell and 1st Lt H A Peters.

Beginning 12 November, the Japanese launched a four-day effort to reinforce the island. Nineteen torpedo-armed 'Bettys' went for US shipping which was unloading off Kukum Point, and the attack was broken up by 15 Wildcats, plus some Army Air Force fighters. Seventeen of the land-attack bombers, plus five Zeros, fell to fighters and flak, mostly accountable to VMF-112 and -121. The low-level combat cost three F4Fs, but the transports continued disembarking troops.

Bearing a black number 29, this VMF-121 F4F-4 taxies on Guadalcanal's pierced-steel matting in November 1942. By that time the squadron had been at 'Cactus' for almost a month. The facility is probably Henderson Field, owing to the SBD and B-17 barely visible in the background. However, F4F operations had previously been moved to an auxiliary field east of Henderson, variously called the 'fighter strip', or more often the 'cow pasture'. The South Pacific climate quickly bleached out aircraft colours, leaving a paler shade than was originally applied. Guadalcanal's alternately muddy and dusty environment, coupled with minimal maintenance facilities, left aircraft with a decidedly 'hang-dog' appearance. Then-Maj Donald K Yost, commanding VMF-121 in early 1943, described it in the following terms;

'The insignia and bright markings designating position in the squadron with which our planes were decorated previously gave way to white or black numbers on the fuselages. Even these numbers were not distinguishing, and usually did not run in sequence. As a result, planes failed to gain an identity. Adding to the anonymity of the F4F-4s which I flew from Guadalcanal were the white airplane-fabric patches glued over numerous bullet holes. Many planes were composites of wings or control surfaces scavenged from wrecked planes, and the whole covered with the mud and dust which seemed ever-present on the fighter strips we flew from in those days'
(via Robert L Lawson)

A VMF-121 aircraft lands at Camp Kearney, later site of Miramar Naval Air Station. Under Capt Leonard K Davis, the squadron operated in the San Diego area from March to August 1942. However, retaining full strength proved almost impossible owing to near-constant transfers of pilots and aircraft to new units. The squadron barely reached operating strength before embarking for the Southwest Pacific. Normal practise on Guadalcanal seldom allowed for individually-assigned aircraft after the early period of the campaign. The usual situation was described by Maj Don Yost;
'The one dereliction from security regulations tactitly permitted was the custom of painting a small Japanese flag on the fuselage below the cockpit for each enemy aircraft destroyed in the air. However, since no plane was regularly assigned to an individual, the plane rather than the pilot was honoured. Because of the limited availability of aircraft, pilots flew any plane that was flyable and loaded for the mission. As a result, a new pilot on his first combat mission might be flying a plane that was well covered with flags'
(via Robert L Lawson)

Two future Medal of Honor winners scored in this fight: Capt Joe Foss, with three kills, and 2nd Lt Jeff DeBlanc, with two, among the total 23 claims. Theirs was a fitting contribution to the Marine Corps' heaviest day of aerial combat in the first year of the war.

The battle continued in Ironbottom Sound that night. An outnumbered American cruiser-destroyer force locked horns with Japanese battleships and other warships, preventing bombardment of Henderson Field. Five US Navy vessels were sunk, as were two Japanese destroyers, while one battleship was crippled.

A misty dawn on the 13th revealed IJNS *Hiei* immobilised and within easy reach of Henderson, which launched SBDs and TBFs to finish her off. Eight defending Zeros were dispersed between 0630 and 0830, elements of three Wildcat squadrons splashing three for the loss of a single F4F, although its pilot was saved.

Meanwhile, *Enterprise* had returned to the area and launched reinforcements for 'Cactus'. Six 'Grim Reapers' arrived with nine VT-10 Avengers in time to celebrate *Hiei's* demise, and to intercept the Japanese troop transports and bombardment group that was steaming rapidly towards Guadalcanal.

'Cactus' was shelled that night, but most rounds fell on the 'Fighter Strip'. Two F4Fs were destroyed and 15 damaged, but by dawn on the 14th there were still 14 operational Wildcats, plus 10 Army fighters. They were all needed as a strong Zero CAP was maintained over 11 troop transports bearing down 'The Slot' toward Guadalcanal's northern coast. The Americans simply could not let additional enemy troops ashore.

While land-based Marine and VF-10 Wildcats fought Zeros and floatplanes over the convoy, *Enterprise* launched additional aircraft. After sinking the cruiser *Kinugasa*, the carrier-based SBDs and F4Fs landed ashore. 'The Big E' retained 18 Wildcats for her own protection – the balance of Air Group 10, however, was now fully committed to 'Cactus'.

Lt Col Joe Bauer, by now working at Fighter Command HQ, stood the inactivity as long as he could. Perhaps nowhere else in the Pacific did so many gifted fighter leaders work so closely as on that day. Flying alongside Bauer were Duke Davis and Joe Foss of VMF-121, plus Jim Flatley of VF-10. After supervising near-constant missions taking off to defeat the Japanese transports, Bauer decided to take a look for himself. That evening he was lost on a strafing mission and eventually received a posthumous Medal of Honor. His citation said in part, 'His intrepid fighting spirit and distinctive ability as a leader and an airman, exemplified in his splendid record of combat achievement, were vital factors in the successful operations in the South Pacific Area.'

Seven of Rear Adm Tanaka's transports were sunk or turned back in the dash for Guadalcanal. In the heaviest day of aerial activity to date, 'Cactus' had launched 86 Navy, Marine and Army bomber sorties, plus 42 Wildcats. Of the latter, VMF-112 was most heavily engaged. However, *Enterprise* fighter pilots were also heard from, including the redoubtable team of Lt Jock Sutherland and Lt(jg) Henry Carey, both veterans of Midway and Santa Cruz.

In exchange for 30 enemy aircraft claimed shot down, the 'CAF' lost two F4Fs and five SBDs. Japanese claims matched the US total, while their own casualties were 12 Zeros and three floatplanes.

When the four surviving transports beached themselves on the morning of the 15th, the Guadalcanal campaign had peaked. Aerial combat quickly abated, as that day involved only two combats with a combined eight claims by VF-10 and VMF-121. In fact, no further Navy victory claims would be made until the end of January.

1942 IN REVIEW

The Pacific Theatre – by far the largest in World War 2 – produced its own band of 'few' fighter pilots. However, the Pacific 'Few' were even fewer than those in RAF Fighter Command in 1940! In fact, their numbers were directly inverse to the time and area involved. From December 1941 through June 1942, the five Navy fighter squadrons' frontline strength totalled only 138 aircrew. For the remainder of the year, 50 of those veterans, and 136 others, bore the burden of the Guadalcanal battles. Thus, the US Navy fought the first 12 months of the Pacific War with 224 combat fighter pilots.

Of these, 27 were killed in action or accidents through to July, with another 31 lost through to November, plus two captured. The total of 60 casualties among frontline Navy fighter pilots equated to a 27 per cent loss rate. Obviously, the Guadalcanal campaign inflicted greater attrition – one out of three pilots engaged were killed. This was to be expected from the grinding, sustained, pace of operations, compared to the sporadic, tentative, nature of the carrier war over the first six months since the Pearl Harbor raid.

Two Marine squadrons committed about 40 pilots at Wake and Midway. The 'Cactus' contingent added approximately 130 more, with a small degree of duplication among Midway survivors. In whole, or in part, six VMF units flew from Guadalcanal through to November, sustaining some 25 pilots killed. Throughout the six-month campaign, 'Cactus' fighter pilots sustained a 20 per cent loss rate. Battling disease, climate and tenuous supplies, the F4F squadrons were short of everything but targets.

Typical of Guadalcanal's mixed-service operations is this scene, which captures Marine Corps F4F-4s with Army Air Forces P-38Fs, circa November 1942. The Lockheed Lightnings afforded 'Cactus Fighter Command' a much-needed high-altitude capability, but P-38 maintenance remained complicated, leading to a relatively low in-commission rate. The Wildcat's simplicity endeared it to mechanics and pilots alike, while a single underwing drop tank helped offset the type's inherently short range *(via Robert L Lawson)*

VMF-224 was the second Wildcat unit despatched to Guadalcanal, and they arrived on 30 August 1942. Leading the unit into battle was the highly talented Maj Robert E Galer, who soon proved both his ability as a leader and as a fighter pilot of some note. Over the next two months – the hardest fought of the Guadalcanal campaign – Galer's squadron accounted for 61.5 Japanese aircraft, with the major himself downing 14 of this total. He finished fourth in the rankings for the Corps in 1942, and was awarded the Medal of Honor upon his return to the US

Pacific F4F Squadron Scores (from July to December 1942)

VMF-223	134.5	'Cactus'; includes 22.5 by TAD* pilots
VMF-121	119	'Cactus'
VMF-224	61.5	'Cactus'; includes 6.5 by TAD* pilots
VMF-212	57	'Cactus'
VF-5	45	*Saratoga* and 'Cactus'
VF-6	44	*Enterprise*
VF-72	38	*Hornet*
VMF-112	36.5	'Cactus'
VF-10	31	*Enterprise* and 'Cactus'
VMO-251	13	'Cactus'
VF-71	7	*Wasp*
VMF-122	5	'Cactus'

*TAD – temporary attached duty from other squadrons

By the end of 1942 the Navy had at least 16 Wildcat aces, who are listed below:

Mach D E Runyon	VF-6	*Enterprise*	8
Lt S W Vejtasa	VF-10	*Enterprise*	7.25
Ens H M Jensen	VF-5	*Saratoga*, Guadalcanal	7
Lt(jg) F R Register	VF-6, -5	*Enterprise*, Guadalcanal	7
Lt(jg) E S McCuskey	VF-42, -3	*Yorktown*	6.50
Lt(jg) A J Brassfield	VF-42, -3	*Yorktown*	6.33
Lt. Cdr J S Thach	VF-3	*Lexington, Yorktown*	6
Ens G L Wrenn	VF-72	*Hornet*	5.25
Ens M K Bright	VF-5	*Saratoga*, Guadalcanal	5
Lt N A M Gayler	VF-3, -2	*Lexington*	5
AP1/c L P Mankin	VF-5, -6	*Saratoga, Enterprise*	5
Lt(jg) E H O'Hare (KIA)	VF-3	*Lexington*	5
Lt(jg) C B Starkes	VF-5	*Saratoga*, Guadalcanal	5
Lt J F Sutherland	VF-72, -10	*Hornet, Enterprise*	5
Lt A O Vorse, Jr	VF-3, -2, -6	*Lexington, Enterprise*	5
Lt(jg) J M Wesolowski	VF-5	*Saratoga*, Guadalcanal	5

Two other F4F pilots deserve a mention; Lt Cdr J H Flatley scored at least four kills while serving as executive officer of VF-42 at Coral Sea and as skipper of VF-10 at Santa Cruz. He may well deserve another victory, but the indefinite phrase 'assist' clouds the matter. Additionally, Lt(jg) W A Haas, of the hard-working VF-42, has a decimal total of 4.83 from the contemporary wartime figure of six victories.

By the end of 1942 the United States Marine Corps had produced 30 aces, all of which are listed below:

Capt J J Foss	VMF-121	23 +3*	2Lt J L Narr	VMF-121	6
Maj J L Smith	VMF-223	19	2Lt Z A Pond	VMF-223	6
Capt M E Carl	VMF-221, -223	16.5	1Lt R F Stout	VMF-224, -212	6
Maj R E Galer	VMF-224	14	2Lt E Trowbridge	VMF-223	6
2Lt K D Frazier	VMF-223	12	Capt D K Yost	VMF-121	6
Lt Col H W Bauer (KIA)	VMF-223, -224, -212	10	Maj F R Payne	VMF-223, -212	5.5
1Lt J E Conger	VMF-223, -212	10	Maj L K Davis	VMF-121	5
Capt L D Everton	VMF-223, -212	10	2Lt C J Doyle (KIA)	VMF-121	5
1Lt W P Marontate (KIA)	VMF-121	10 +3*	1Lt F C Drury	VMF-223, -212	5
2Lt T H Mann	VMF-224, -121	9	Maj P J Fontana	VMF-112	5
2Lt G L Hollowell	VMF-224	8	2Lt C Kendrick (KIA)	VMF-223	5
Maj J F Dobbin	VMF-224	7.5	2Lt H Phillips	VMF-223	5
M G H B Hamilton (KIA)	VMF-223, -212	7	2Lt W B Freeman	VMF-121	5 +1*
2Lt R A Haberman	VMF-121	6.5	2Lt O H Ramlo	VMF-223	5
2Lt C M Kunz	VMF-224	6			
1Lt G K Loesch	VMF-121	6 +2.5*			

*Note – +3, +2.5 or +1 indicates further F4F victories in 1943

ONE MAN'S WAR – A PILOT PROFILE OF
JOSEPH FOSS

Capt Joseph J Foss at the end of his Guadalcanal tour in early 1943. Credited with 26 Japanese aircraft, he was then the leading fighter ace of the United States, and was shortly to be awarded the Medal of Honor – a distinction he shared with seven other F4F pilots. Despite his exceptional combat success as executive officer of VMF-121, Foss suffered from recurring malaria, which would plague him until after the war. Indeed, he was forced to return to the US after embarking on his second combat tour as CO of the F4U-equipped VMF-115 in September 1943 because of illness. Due to a bureaucratic error, Foss was denied a regular commission postwar, so he helped form the South Dakota Air National Guard, logging 1500 happy hours in P-51Ds prior to transitioning to jets. He subsequently attained the rank of brigadier general in the Air Force Reserve, serving a spell as national president of the Air Force Association. Enjoying successful careers in politics, professional sports and commercial aviation, Foss also helped form the American Fighter Aces Association, and recently became president of the National Rifle Association of America
(via Robert L Lawson)

Joseph Jacob Foss was destined to become a hunter. Born to a Norwegian-Scots farming family in South Dakota in 1915, he learned early in life the principles of stalking and marksmanship. Combined with a childhood passion for aviation, perhaps it was inevitable that he would become a fighter pilot. The same Scandinavian heritage and rural upbringing led to similar success among others of his generation: Richard Bong, Marion Carl and Stanley Vejtasa, to name but a few.

Like millions of his generation, 11-year-old Joe was inspired by Charles Lindbergh's transatlantic flight in 1927. The future ace's first flight occurred with his father as paying customers in a barnstorming Ford Trimotor. Though Frank Foss died while Joe was in high school, the youngster persisted in his dream of flying. And his ambition became focused when a squadron of Marine Corps biplanes passed through Sioux Falls in 1930. The excitement and glamour of fighters capable of landing on aircraft carriers planted a seed in Joe Foss that would germinate in years to come. Leader of the formation was Capt Clayton C Jerome, later wartime Director of Marine Corps Aviation.

Foss realised that any hope of a career in the military depended upon a college education. It was a major challenge for a financially-strapped farm family during the depression of the 1930s. As a part-time college student he accumulated enough credits to enter the University of South Dakota in 1939. While there he scraped up enough money to complete a private-pilot's course. Then, eternally optimistic, Foss hitch-hiked 300 miles to Minneapolis, Minnesota, to apply for the naval aviation cadet programme. Of 28 applicants, he was one of two chosen. Upon graduation in June 1940 he reported to Chamberlain Field in Minneapolis for elimination flight training.

Foss' prior experience apparently helped, as he survived the 12-hour 'E base' curriculum. He then proceeded to NAS Pensacola, and following seven months further training, was commissioned as a second lieutenant in the 'Corps. However, he had barely pinned on his coveted wings of gold when he learned that he would become a 'plowback' instructor, remaining at Pensacola for the next nine months. He was not pleased.

Foss was officer of the day on 7 December 1941. The base commander, a Navy captain, pointed at the 26-year-old lieutenant and, in so many words, said, 'You're in charge'. Foss admits that he swallowed hard, replied, 'Yes, sir!' and prepared to defend NAS Pensacola from Japanese commandos. He spent the first day of the war on a bicycle, arranging for security of the perimeter!

New Year's Day 1942 brought cheerier prospects, but only barely. Delighted to be heading closer to the war – NAS San Diego, California – he was distressed at his orders to report to VMO-1, a photo-reconnaissance squadron. At that point Foss demonstrated early signs of the initiative that would take him to the top of the list of Marine Corps aces. Determined to get into fighters, he began a calculated campaign to overcome the anti-Marine bias of the commanding officer of Aircraft Carrier Training Group (ACTG). At first progress was slow, which is to say non-existent. Though new Marine Corps squadrons were forming at nearby

Kearney Field (now NAS Miramar), there was little need for aspiring F4F pilots in ACTG. Like a patient hunter, Foss bided his time.

Then he hit upon a plan. Overhearing some Navy pilots complaining about the mortality rate in carrier training, Foss decided to take advantage of the situation. He told the CO that he would volunteer for the funeral detail in exchange for a cockpit seat in ACTG. His earnestness won out, and Foss began a cram course on the Wildcat, aerial gunnery and carrier procedures. He still credits the instruction he received at ACTG for much of his later success, especially the patient tutelage of Lt Edward Pawka, who would finish the war as an air group commander.

However, Foss was a more than willing pupil. In seven weeks during June and July, he logged 156 flight hours – an incredible average of more than three hours per day for 47 days. With that kind of experience, Foss was noticed, and on 1 August he was assigned to VMF-121, becoming executive officer to Capt Leonard K Davis – a product of the Annapolis class of 1935.

Over the next two weeks it became obvious that the unit would shortly be sent to a combat zone. Therefore, while time allowed, Foss married a former Sioux Falls schoolmate, but there was no opportunity for a honeymoon. Promoted to captain, he barely had time to pin on his new bars before VMF-121 embarked in the liner *Matsonia*, destination unknown.

The destination did not remain a secret for long. Arriving in the Southwest Pacific, VMF-121 was loaded aboard the escort carrier *Copahee*. Twenty Wildcats were catapulted off the morning of 9 October. It would be Foss' only combat mission from a carrier deck, but his arduous work at ACTG back in San Diego had paid off. Landing at Henderson Field, the newcomers were told that their fighters were now based at the nearby 'cow pasture', one mile east. Another fighter strip was under construction to the west, near Kukum Point.

Looking around, Foss was impressed with the make-do nature of the 'Cactus Air Force'. Henderson was riddled with bomb craters, and wrecked aircraft were strewn about, awaiting collection. However, there were also two radar stations and three batteries of big 90 mm anti-aircraft guns in the vicinity. VMF-121 had arrived just in time, as the remnants of John L Smith's -223 flew their last 'Cactus' mission the next day.

As 'exec', Foss led a flight of two four-fighter divisions whenever eight Wildcats were available to him. His pilots included six second lieutenants and a flying sergeant, who all averaged out at 23 years of age. Foss, at 27, was the old man of the flight. Collectively known as 'Foss' Flying Circus', the flight would be credited with 61.5 victories, and four others besides Foss would become aces. Two of them would be lost in action, however.

Foss flew several F4F-4s at Guadalcanal, without one permanently assigned. Most of VMF-121's aircraft used white numbers on wings and fuselage, and Foss arrived in number 13. This was quickly changed to 53 to avoid duplication with another F4F, but he has also been identified with numbers 50 and 84.

At noon on 13 October, VMF-121 scored its first victories as an independent squadron. Second Lts William B Freeman and Joseph L Narr, both future aces, claimed a bomber and a Zero, respectively. Later that afternoon Foss led a dozen F4Fs to intercept 14 twin-engined bombers escorted by 18 Zeros. In his first combat, Foss was jumped by a Zero which overshot his F4F and pulled up ahead of him. He got in a good burst at the enemy fighter and claimed it destroyed. In moments, however, he was beset by three more, which shot out his oil cooler. When his engine seized, Foss poked the Grumman's nose down and screeched into a rough, bumpy, landing at 'Fighter One'. He said that he learned a vital lesson from this first sortie, vowing that from then on, 'The boys could call me "Swivel-Neck Joe"'.

Foss' first dogfight established a pattern. He became a rough-and-tumble fighter along the lines of Joe Bauer. Though he seldom returned from combat without bullet holes in his F4F, he still believed in getting in close – so close, in fact, that another pilot joked that the 'exec' left powder burns on his targets.

Foss got his next chance the following afternoon. Composition of the Japanese formation was similar to the day before: 12 bombers with 15 fighters. As the Mitsubishis split to bomb both airfields, VF-5 waded into them from a better altitude. However, Foss' F4F lagged behind the others and he had to be satisfied with picking off a Zero which dived after a Marine Wildcat. Another of his flight, Master Sgt J J Palko, claimed a twin-engined reconnaissance plane. VMF-121 lost an F4F and its pilot.

Though air defence was the Wildcats' primary role, other missions arose. When ammunition supply permitted, fighters often strafed Japanese positions, rather than take a full .50-cal load back to the 'Fighter Strip'. On other occasions the F4Fs ranged farther afield. At dawn on the 16th Foss led a strafing mission, shooting up landing craft near Kokumbona. Diving through AA fire, the Wildcats inflicted heavy losses on Japanese infantry, but one pilot failed to return.

Though holding their own in the air, the fighter pilots spent long, arduous, nights on the ground. During mid-October enemy warships bombarded Henderson Field and the surrounding area three nights running. Some fliers resorted to the desperate method of trying to sleep near the frontlines, south of the field.

After his first few combats, Foss grew more appreciative of the fighter doctrine handed down from the Navy. He held that, 'Looking around doesn't cost anything and is a healthy habit for pilots to develop'. He also found the 'Thach-Flatley' weave (the name was a misnomer) a near-perfect method of countering the Zero's superior performance because, as he said many times, 'It allowed us to point eyes and guns in every direction'.

Following a large interception on the morning of 18 October, Foss was leading another flight outbound when the Zero top cover descended. Though a trailing F4F went down, Foss' flight turned the tables and caught three Zeros from above. He flamed the nearest, hit another which made off trailing smoke, and then fought a short battle with the third. Finally, gaining an angle, he drew lead and fired, setting the engine alight.

Next, Foss latched onto a group of bombers already under attack by VF-71. Though identified as twin-tailed types, they were familiar 'Bettys' from the Misawa Naval Air Group. Foss hit one, then dived below the formation and pulled up steeply. Firing almost vertically, he saw his bullets destroy one engine. The Mitsubishi dropped out of formation and later crashed in 'The Slot'. Nine days after landing at Guadalcanal, Joe Foss was an ace.

On the morning of the 20th Lt Col Joe Bauer, running 'Cactus Fighter

Command', sent Foss off with seven F4Fs to intercept 15 Zeros, the latter being ably supported by Maj Davis and his section of eight Wildcats. In a close, manoeuvring, combat, Foss claimed two kills. Then another Zero put 7.7 mm rounds into his engine. As he had done on his first mission, Foss force-landed back on his airfield, though this time in a more controlled fashion than before. One Marine pilot was lost to Zeros.

With advance knowledge of a Japanese build-up, 'Fighter Command' kept as many Wildcats available as maintenance allowed. On the 23rd VMF-121 was up in strength as Davis and Foss each had their flights airborne. With Zeros and bombers overhead, there was no shortage of targets. Both flights engaged. Foss' first opportunity was a Zero tearing after an F4F, firing with all guns. Foss closed in, clamped down on the trigger and the Zero exploded. Next, he tagged onto another which attempted to evade in a loop. Foss had never been taught to shoot while inverted, but he followed and caught the Japanese pulling over the top. He described it as a lucky shot, but flamed his victim nonetheless.

Nosing down to regain airspeed, Foss spotted an exuberant Zero pilot performing a slow roll. It was a quick set-up, but Foss put his gunsight on the fighter as its wings rolled through the vertical and fired. He gazed in amazement at the spectacle of the enemy aviator blown out of his cockpit, minus his parachute. Without time to reorient himself, the lone Marine was aware of other aircraft falling around him – Duke Davis' flight was obviously doing its job overhead. However, a brace of Zeros then sandwiched Foss between them. Trusting in the Grumman Iron Works, he pressed home his run on the frontmost Zero. Both pilots fired and both scored, but Foss' superior armament made the difference. Passing off his port wingtip, the Zero came apart in flames.

He emptied his guns at another bandit, then realized that the fourth Japanese had hit him. With smoke streaming from his abused Pratt & Whitney, Foss followed previous procedure and began a long glide toward home. When he landed the battered Wildcat he had raised his tally to 11 victories, but reminded himself that this was the fourth F4F he had returned too damaged to fly again. Nevertheless, VMF-121 had claimed 11 of the day's 22 kills credited to 'Corps pilots – the balance going to VMF-212.

On 25 October Japanese naval, air and ground forces expected to occupy Henderson Field, and the F4F pilots were beneficiaries of the action. Presaging the carrier battle off Santa Cruz the next day, Zero fighter sweeps capped 'Cactus' throughout the morning. Their orders: circle for upwards of four hours, then land when it was clear the Imperial Army owned the place.

Joe Foss had other ideas. Before 1000 he led six Wildcats off the 'Fighter Strip' and tangled with the first wave of nine Zeros. Fighting their way upward from only 1500 ft, the Marines claimed three victories for one F4F lost. Foss was credited with two of the kills but later berated himself for wasting ammunition in long-range shooting. After a few missions he learned the value of getting close and firing short bursts. Later, whilst touring training bases he told aviation cadets that he lost four certain kills because of poor fire discipline.

Subsequently, a VMF-212 division tangled with intrusive Zeros, then Foss was up again. He led an eclectic bunch – his wingman, Oscar Bate, plus three VF-71 pilots, putting their skills to use after *Wasp* was torpedoed and sunk on 15 September. They tangled with a potent *chutai*: six fighters of the Tainan Air Group flown by experienced pilots, including two aces. For once the F4Fs had the altitude advantage, allowing Foss to start the fight by gunning one Zero from astern. Then the other five A6Ms bounced the diving Grummans.

Foss was attacked by a Zero which fired at him and missed. Reversing hard to starboard, the Marine was now on the A6M's tail and shooting before the Japanese could evade. The enemy pilot bailed out seconds before the Zero exploded. Low on ammunition, Foss turned for home. However, he noticed two Zeros stalking another F4F and shouted a warning. His radio call saved the Wildcat, but both A6Ms then turned on him. Foss ducked into a cloud, reversed course and emerged to find one of the stalkers under his guns. Closing in to be sure, he destroyed the Zero with his remaining ammunition.

With five victories in two take-offs, Foss had become the first Marine Corps ace in a day. Proud of his accomplishment, he boasted to Lt Doyle, 'That was one hop I didn't get any bullet holes in my plane'. Doyle, seizing an opportunity, pointed to the dimpled armour plate behind Foss' headrest. 'What do you call those?', he retorted.

The Navy-Marine F4Fs claimed four victories from this fight, and in fact got three. Moreover, Foss had made 14 claims in 13 days. He was running at a rate that was even in advance of Smith and Carl – the latter had actually been one of Foss' instructors at Pensacola.

Despite almost daily flights with frequent combat and perennial bombing and shelling, Foss retained his stamina and enthusiasm. Not content with playing the fighter pilot role, he and some other VMF-121 stalwarts occasionally borrowed rifles and went prowling in the jungle – however, Lt Col Joe Bauer promptly put an end to that sport, as trained fighter pilots were virtually irreplaceable.

Though very crude, living facilities on Guadalcanal had improved from the early days of the late summer. Pilots slept in six-man tents and ate dehydrated eggs for breakfast under a tarp. Somebody had a scratchy old gramophone which played worn-out records of popular songs, and outdated magazines were available. Bathing facilites were basic, but effective – the nearby Lunga River. Many pilots grew short beards, as it was more convenient than shaving in cold water. However, they learned to keep the beards trimmed because facial hair could interfere with the proper fit of an oxygen mask.

'Washing Machine Charlie' and 'Millimeter Mike' were the generic names which Marines assigned to harassing enemy night fliers and hidden artillery pieces which shelled the airfields. Therefore, some pilots tried sleeping during the day. However, since two patrols a day were common, to say nothing of unexpected scrambles, a 'combat nap' was a catch-as-catch-can affair.

After 11 days of relative inactivity, Foss was shooting again on 7 November. Late that afternoon he led seven F4Fs against Japanese warships steaming down 'The Slot'. In one of the largest reinforcement efforts yet, a cruiser and nine destroyers were covered by six Zero floatplanes ('Rufes') which had attacked a formation of VMF-112 Wildcats. As Foss related later, 'Somebody was going to get left out'. He downed one A6M2N, pulled around for a shot at another and saw his wingman, 2nd Lt 'Boot' Furlow, flame the last one. When Foss looked around for another target, he observed the eerie spectacle of five empty parachutes.

Preparing to strafe the ships, Foss threw a cautionary glance over his shoulder. There was at least one other floatplane among the clouds, so he climbed into position and initiated a high-side run. Only as he closed did he discern it was a biplane – undoubtedly an F1M2 'Pete'. With excessive speed, Foss passed close aboard when the sharpshooting rear-seat man opened fire. Several bullets struck Foss' airframe, with one 7.7 mm round starring the portside glass of his windscreen.

Foss decided to respect the enemy's ability. Approaching for a pass from below, he put a telling burst into the starboard wingroot. The 'Pete' dropped away as Foss noticed another Mitsubishi. He repeated the successful low astern approach and ignited the floatplane in one pass.

En route home, Foss encountered a series of line squalls. He diverted around some of the clouds, but when he broke into the clear he realised he was off course. Then his engine began cutting out. Apparently the Japanese gunner had inflicted serious damage, as the R1830 began trailing smoke, then cut out completely.

He mothered the doomed Wildcat, stretching his glide as much as he dared. He had sight of land ahead and steered for it. It proved to be Malaita, the long, thin, island east of Guadalcanal. The ensuing water landing was rough and bumpy, being performed more than two miles offshore. As the F4F rapidly sank nose first, Foss struggled with his parachute harness. Then, with one foot caught under the seat, he went down with his aircraft. As it sank, Foss struggled for air. In desperation, he gulped in saltwater. He realised that he was close to drowning.

Fighting panic, Foss forced himself to concentrate. He talked himself through the escape and, once loose in the cockpit, he inflated his Mae West. From approximately 30 ft he was carried upward, inhaling more water in the process. Upon breaking the surface, Foss was exhausted. The tide was against him and he knew it was useless to try swimming to shore. Therefore, he kicked off his shoes and tried to float on his back. He wanted to rest and regain his strength before trying anything else. However, future plans were chillingly interrupted when one or two shark fins sliced through the water nearby. He spread his chlorine capsule around him and that seemed to help.

By dark, Foss was no closer to land. However, some canoes came out from shore, obviously looking for him. Foss lay still in the water, half convinced they were Japanese, when he heard someone say, 'Let's look over here'. The searchers turned out to be planters and mill workers. They hauled him aboard with his waterlogged parachute and took him home.

'Home' proved to be a large mission, complete with two bishops. Additionally, there were Australians, Europeans and even two Americans. One of the nuns had been on Malaita 40 years and had never seen an automobile. The first aeroplanes she had seen were Japanese. That night Foss dined on steak and eggs. His hosts invited him to stay for two weeks, but the errant ace explained how he had a pressing previous commitment. He accepted their hospitality overnight, being buzzed by a VMF-121 Wildcat in the process.

On the eighth, a PBY Catalina landed and taxied up to shore. Foss, dressed only in worn-out trousers and stockings, scrambled aboard. All the way back he chatted with the pilot, longtime friend Maj J R 'Mad Jack' Cram, who updated Foss on 'Cactus' gossip.

Upon returning to Guadalcanal, Foss was told that Fighter Command had claimed 15 enemy aircraft on the seventh. His own three victories raised his tally to 19, tying him with Maj Smith of VMF-223. However, there was also grim news – five-kill ace 2nd Lt Danny Doyle was missing in action. He was last seen chasing an enemy aircraft on the day Foss went down. No trace of him was ever found.

Back only one day, Foss received the Distinguished Flying Cross from Vice Adm William F Halsey, the theatre commander, on 9 November 1942. Also decorated were 2nd Lts W B 'Whiskey Bill' Freeman and Wallace G Wethe, also of VMF-121. Two days later, Foss was back in action. However, he missed both interceptions on 11 November when VMF-121 lost four pilots, plus Maj Davis and one other slightly wounded. Foss had much better luck on the 12th.

That morning Rabaul launched a major effort against four US transports unloading Army troops at Lunga Roads. Sixteen 'Bettys' and 30 Zeros strobed on 'Cactus' radar early in the afternoon, and the ships withdrew to the channel where they could maneouvre. Meanwhile, Foss was airborne with eight Wildcats, supported by an equal number of P-39 Airacobras. Taking advantage of low clouds, the attackers got in beneath the CAP, but were immediately beset by VMF-112. Foss' top-cover flight then screamed to wavetop level to help. This descent was performed at as fast a velocity as Foss ever achieved in a F4F. Whatever the actual speed, his full-power dive was so rapid that his windscreen iced up in the warmer, lower, air, and his canopy burst from the increasing pressure. Other Wildcats lost inspection panels in the headlong plunge.

Foss and his pilots chased the speedy Mitsubishis into a cloud of American flak, descending to 50 ft or less. Ignoring the peril, Foss hauled into within 100 yards of the nearest bomber and aimed at the starboard engine, which spouted flame. The G4M tried a water landing, caught a wingtip and tumbled into oblivion. Foss set his sight on another 'Betty' when a Zero intervened. The F4F nosed up briefly and fired a beautifully-aimed snapshot which sent the A6M spearing into the water. He then resumed the chase.

Setting up to starboard, Foss tracked the next 'Betty' in line and fired, but missed. Still low, he was concerned about being trapped by other Zeros. However, he passed to port and made a deflection shot which connected with the 'Betty's' wingroot. Flames spread along the wing and the bomber made a controlled water landing. As he passed over the sinking bomber, Foss noted that the enemy tail gunner hosed off an angry burst as a parting shot. Overhauling another 'Betty', the Marine fired and saw strikes, but inflicted no significant damage. At that point two more Zeros joined the fight, forcing Foss to break off. He steered his F4F in the direction of Savo Island, where a P-39 crossed his flight path, intent on yet another bomber.

Out of ammunition and low on fuel, Foss turned for home. However, other Japanese fighters remained in the area, and he dodged one persistent Zero before eluding it in the clouds.

Through a combination of US fighters and flak, the American warships escaped serious damage, and none of the aerial torpedoes found their intended targets. Total F4F credits amounted to 16 bombers and seven Zeros. In fact five of the 16 'Bettys' that returned to base never flew again. Though only one Zero was known to be lost, US fighters had clearly mastered the situation. Rabaul's A6Ms could no longer protect the bombers. From this combat Foss' tally rose to 22, the first time an American pilot had achieved such a score in World War 2.

That night, Foss sat out the surface engagement raging in Ironbottom Sound. From their living area under the palm trees, aviators heard gunfire and occasionally saw muzzle flashes or exploding shells. An outgunned Allied cruiser-destroyer force prevented yet another Japanese bombardment, but at a high cost – two destroyers sunk on the spot and three more dead in the water. Two cruisers had received serious damage while the task-force commanders, Rear Adms Callaghan and Scott, had both been killed in the clash.

Foss was airborne soon after dawn on the 13th, scouting the area for an expected Japanese landing. However, the naval 'slugfest' had prevented enemy troopships from continuing southward. Beyond Savo Island, Foss was treated to the unexpected sight of a crippled enemy battleship, unable to steam clear of danger. Later in the day Foss and company covered Navy and Marine bombers and torpedo planes which were sent out to destroy HIJMS *Hiei* – she duly became the first Japanese battleship sunk in World War 2.

More Japanese shipping was on the way. Search aircraft on the morning of 14 November brought word of a major reinforcement convoy: 11 troop ships and 12 escorts. Bearing 7000 fresh infantry, the convoy had to be stopped. The 'Cactus Air Force' began a day-long series of flights aimed at sinking Rear Adm Raizo Tanaka's command.

After co-ordinating fighter escorts all day, Lt Col Bauer decided to take a look for himself. Attached to Foss and Lt Furlow that evening, he participated in a strafing mission against the convoy, which was passing the Russell Islands. They pressed their attacks almost to wavetop level, strafing packed decks full of enemy soldiers. Pulling away, Foss and Bauer were alerted of danger by tracers flashing past. Looking back, Foss saw two Zeros descending and, with Bauer, turned into the threat. Bauer took one head-on and shot it into the water – his tenth confirmed kill.

Foss and Furlow went after the other, which eluded them in the crisscrossing tracers over the convoy. The two Marines reversed course, looking to rejoin Bauer but could not find his aircraft. Then Foss noticed an oil slick near the Zero's crash site. Circling low, he saw Joe Bauer afloat in his Mae West, waving animatedly toward Henderson Field. It was not clear whether the doomed Zero had hit Bauer's engine or whether 'The Coach' had been knocked down by AA gunners. In any event, Foss tried to radio for help but could not get through. With a dip of his wing, he rolled out on a return course and sped for home in the gathering dusk.

Foss' main concern was daylight, which was fast fading. Knowing he stood little chance of finding Bauer after dark, he landed, scrambled out of his F4F and found another operations officer, Maj Joe Renner. Immediately he led Foss to a Grumman J2F amphibian and hopped into the cockpit. With Foss in the passenger's seat, Bauer's friends raced back to 'The Slot' as fast as the Duck would take them. They were escorted by two

Capt Joe Foss pensively stares off into the middle distance, his weary fatigues perhaps best illustrating the strain that he, and every other 'Corps pilot in-theatre, had been subjected to for the previous six months. This photograph was just one of dozens taken by the Marine Corps for publicity purposes in the weeks after Foss had beaten Eddie Rickenbacker's 26-kill record from World War 1

'Joe's Flying Circus' in February 1943. Foss, on the far left, poses on a specially-marked Wildcat with the seven other members of his flight. The name *Marine Special* on the cowling appears to be painted in white block letters. Such non-regulation adornments were unusual on Guadalcanal during the campaign, but became somewhat more common after the island was declared secure
(via Robert L Lawson)

rapidly-drafted Wildcat escorts from VMF-112 and -121.

In full darkness, little was visible other than five burning ships. Renner flew low, criss-crossing the combat area, but neither he nor Foss could see anyone in the water. Deeply concerned, Renner considered a water landing to wait out the night, but Foss realised that with more enemy fleet units approaching, 'The Slot' was no place for an ungainly biplane. With growing apprehension they reluctantly turned for home, determined to return at first light.

They made the right decision. Another surface engagement flared up that night, costing the Japanese another battleship and several destroyers while the US Navy lost three destroyers. At dawn on the 15th, Tanaka's three surviving transports ran themselves aground on Guadalcanal's northern coast. Only one of the remaining destroyers managed to put any troops ashore.

The tireless Joe Renner was back in his Duck, protected by Foss with eight Wildcats. Ordinarily, Foss would have grounded himself – he was running a 103-degree temperature – but everyone at 'Cactus' wanted to retrieve 'The Coach'. Determined to pick up Bauer, or any other American flier they could find, the rescuers ran into like-minded enemy aviators. While Renner tried to stay out of the way, Foss and Lt Oscar Bate each splashed a 'Jake' floatplane. The gunner in Foss' Aichi fired all the way down, leaving the fighter ace with an abiding respect for Japanese aircrews. No trace of Lt Col Harold Bauer was ever found .

Back on the ground, Foss was diagnosed with advanced malaria. His flight was taken over by 2nd Lt Bill Marontate, already credited with ten victories. Foss hardly noticed the passage of time. Despite quinine medication, he lapsed in and out of awareness.

With the destruction of the Japanese convoy, the worst was over for 'Cactus'. On 19 November Foss felt well enough to join several other VMF-121 pilots in New Caledonia. Still groggy and achy, he had lost 37 lbs on Guadalcanal. On the 30th Davis' veterans proceeded to Sydney, Australia, and revelled in the near-forgotten luxury of civilisation.

Whilst there, Foss met the leading Australian fighter aces, Wg Cdr Clive R Caldwell and Sqn Ldr Keith W Truscott. Foss judged 'Killer' and 'Bluey' as 'good blokes', but he noticed a disturbing attitude among some veterans of the European and North African campaigns, who seemed to regard the Japanese as second-rate opponents. Despite Foss' record of 23 credited victories, when he expressed the opinion that a lone F4F was outclassed by a single Zero, some of his hosts openly scoffed. A few weeks later, trying to fight a turning battle in their Spitfires, they belatedly learned that the brash American knew whereof he spoke.

Headed back to combat in mid-December, Foss was waylaid at New Caledonia with a relapse of malaria. He spent Christmas dinner with a hospitable French family who spoke no English, but enjoyed the sumptuous meal just the same. Then, flying overnight, he landed on Guadalcanal early on New Year's Day 1943.

Foss quickly settled back into the routine of bombings and shellings, though improvements had been made in his six-week absence. The 'Fighter Strip' now boasted steel planking, and the operations office was run by Lt Col Sam Jack, VMF-121's original commanding officer.

However, the pace of operations was such that Jack needed some help.

Therefore, Foss filled the morning of 15 January by arranging for fighter escort of strikes against Japanese ships near the Russells. However, he was airborne that same afternoon with seven F4Fs as top cover for SBDs. Bill Marontate saw some square-winged Zeros (later called 'Hamps') and took his division down to engage. Four kills were scored, including one by Marontate – his 13th. However, he then apparently collided with a 'Hamp', as he was seen falling minus one wing. Though somebody reported seeing a pilot successfully bail out of a stricken Wildcat, Marontate never returned. He remained VMF-121's second-ranking ace.

In the ensuing combat, Foss tried a snapshot at one A6M and missed. Another dived in front of him, but this time his aim was dead on: the 'Hamp' exploded. Almost immediately an F4F crossed his nose with a Mitsubishi in tow. Foss fired almost reflexively, not expecting results, but when he looked back the fighter was falling in flames.

Next, Foss jumped a Zero dogging Oscar Bate's tail. Realising its peril, the A6M reversed into the threat. Both pilots fired from close range, but apparently neither scored. Foss could see the Japanese aviator in the cockpit, even noting the anti-glare panel in front of the windscreen.

Twice more the Mitsubishi and Grumman passed one another, firing repeatedly. Foss recognized his opponent as skilled and aggressive, describing this combat as 'one of the most nerve-wracking situations I was ever in'. Following the third set of scissors, Foss was ready to disengage owing to other Zeros in the area. As he glanced back, he saw his antagonist circling below and beginning to trail flames. Foss then ducked into a cloud, happy to be alone. When he emerged, Foss rejoined on Bate and returned to base. Dodging fresh craters in the runway, they landed with bombs falling all around them.

Foss' last mission at Guadalcanal was flown 10 days later. He led his flight, and four P-38s, to intercept a large Japanese force of Zeros and 'Vals' estimated to number more than 60 aircraft. Rather than be drawn into combat by some tempting Zeros which he recognised as bait, Foss elected to maintain altitude and position. Prolonged sparring with the A6Ms allowed 'Cactus' to scramble additional fighters which dealt with the raiders. In one of the war's ironies, during Joe Foss' most satisfying mission he fired not one round.

On 26 January Foss, and most of the other VMF-121 veterans, left Guadalcanal, bound for home. He arrived by ship on 19 April, still showing the effects of malaria. By the time he was reunited with his wife in Washington, DC, Foss realised that he was about to begin 'the dancing bear act'. He learned that he was the first American fighter pilot to equal the Great War record of Capt Eddie Rickenbacker – that feat was to act as a springboard to the rest of his life.

The 'backbone' of VMF-121 pose for an informal group shot in late October 1942. From left to right, the pilots are 2nd Lt Roger A Haberman (6.5 kills), 2nd Lt Cecil J 'Danny' Doyle (5 kills), Capt Joe Foss (26 kills), 1st Lt W P Marontate (13 kills) and 2nd Lt Roy M Ruddell (3 kills) – their individually tailored attire emphasises the 'make do' nature of the campaign. 'Danny' Doyle was killed on 7 November 1942, and Bill Marontate was lost following a collision with a 'Hamp' on 15 January 1943, his F4F being seen to plunge seaward minus one wing

This portrait of Foss, taken on 20 March 1943 (almost two months after his final mission over Guadalcanal), shows him in his dress uniform en route to the US. It was taken during VMF-121's brief period of R&R in Hawaii

A WARTIME HISTORY OF VMF-121

Marine Fighting Squadron 121 (VMF-121) was established at Quantico, Virginia on 24 June 1941. The unit was still absorbing 21 F4F-3s on 7 December when Maj Samuel J Jack hastily recalled his command from various outlying fields and, four days later, arrived in San Diego, California. Following expansion and transition to F4F-4s at Camp Kearney (now NAS Miramar), Jack turned the unit over to Capt Leonard K Davis in March 1942. Embarking for the South Pacific with other elements of Marine Air Group 14, VMF-121 arrived at New Caledonia in August – just in time to prepare for events at Guadalcanal.

On 26 September Davis – now a major – sent five pilots to 'Cactus', where they were temporarily attached to VMF-223 or -224. Whilst on Guadalcanal, two of the detached pilots scored four-and-a-half victories. They were soon reinforced as the rest of the pilots arrived on 9 October, followed by the ground echelon four days later. Operating from 'Fighter Strip One', VMF-121 immediately began taking a toll of the enemy.

The squadron's best day in combat occurred on 25 October, with 18 shootdowns credited. Capt Foss claimed five Zeros in two missions, while Davis became an ace with victories over a Zero and a 'Val'. Probably the hardest day of battle was 11 November when VMF-121 lost six aircraft and four pilots against 10 victories during enemy attacks on US shipping.

Davis remained in command until 16 December, well after the crisis had passed at Guadalcanal. He was relieved by Maj Donald K Yost on New Year's Day, who was in turn succeed by Maj Joseph N Renner and Ray L Vroome.

VMF-121 continued flying F4F-4s until the spring of 1943. At that time, after 161.5 victory claims in Wildcats, the squadron transitioned to F4U-1 Corsairs. Not only was that figure the highest in the Marine Corps to date, but it also remained tops for all Navy and USMC Wildcat squadrons as well. The squadron's first combat in Corsairs occurred on the morning of 12 June when, in a dogfight over the Russells, five pilots claimed six confirmed and four probable Zeros.

The squadron's best day in F4Us occurred on 30 June 1943 in a series of combats over, and around, Rendova. Throughout the morning and afternoon constant CAPs were flown in the area, resulting in claims for 16 Zeros and three probables, plus three 'Bettys' destroyed. From these combats emerged VMF-121's first F4U ace, Capt Kenneth M Ford. Two days later, again over Rendova, VMF-121 confirmed its last Corsair aces: Capts Robert M Baker and Perry L Shuman. In all, 40+ shootdowns were credited through July, with a dozen VMF-121 aces having been placed on the roster since October 1942.

After three combat tours in the Solomons the veteran unit returned to the US, settling at MCAS Mojave, California, in October. At that time Capt Quintus B Nelson began 'turn-around' training in preparation for another overseas deployment.

By October 1941 three of the Marine Corps' four fighting squadrons operated F4Fs – VMF-111 and -121 (pictured) with Marine Air Group One at Quantico, Virginia, and VMF-211 at Ewa, Hawaii. The fourth unit, VMF-221, flew Brewster F2A Buffaloes at San Diego, California. This pale-grey Wildcat carries white side markings showing 121-MF-?, the individual aircraft number unfortunately being obscured by the wing. The squadron emerged from World War 2 as the Marine Corps' top-scoring fighter unit *(via Robert L Lawson)*

Maj Walter J Meyer became the tenth CO on 1 December, and remained in command until May 1945, far longer than any of VMF-121's other wartime leaders. By July 1944 the squadron was headed back into combat, returning to Espiritu Santo in early August. Preceded by the ground echelon to Peleliu Atoll in the Palaus, the Corsairs landed on 25 October – the second anniversary of Joe Foss' five-kill day. Once established at Peleliu, VMF-121 began a lengthy series of fighter-bomber strikes against Yap Atoll in the Carolines. While the unit was based at Ulithi Atoll, 1st Lts H H Hill and G C Huntington teamed up to shoot down a 'Myrt' recce-aircraft on 28 April. It was -121's first victory in 21 months, and it proved to be their last of the war.

From May through to July the squadron was led by Majs Claude H Welch and Robert Tucker, before 1st Lt R M Loughery took over on 1 August. Two weeks later Japan agreed to surrender and, on 1 September, -121 embarked for America. At war's end VMF-121 was easily the top-scoring fighter squadron in the Marine Corps. Though aerial opposition was virtually non-existent on its second tour, the 1942-43 era in the Solomons brought the squadron 208 credited victories – well ahead of second-place VMF-221 with 185 shootdowns.

VMF-121 received two decorations during the war: the Presidential Unit Citation for Guadalcanal from August to December 1942, and the Navy Unit Commendation for Peleliu and the Western Carolines from September 1944 to January 1945. The 14 fighter aces produced by the unit remained the record for the Marine Corps.

VMF-121's 'ready room' at Guadalcanal. Between scrambles and scheduled patrols, the open-air environment lent itself to cards and checkers, as seen here. Sitting at the table, left to right, are Lts J L Narr and F C Drury, Maj L K Davis, and Lts G K Loesch and J A Stubb. Kibbitzers are Maj P J Fontana (CO VMF-112) and Lt Finney, an intelligence officer. Narr, Drury, Davis, Loesch and Fontana all became fighter aces
(via Robert L Lawson)

VMF-121 Aces

Maj Joseph J Foss	26	Medal of Honor
1Lt William P Marontate	13	KIA 15 January 1943
Capt Gregory K Loesch	8.5	KIA September 1943
2Lt Joseph L Narr	7	
2Lt Roger A Haberman	6.5	
2Lt William B Freeman	6	
Capt Francis E Pierce, Jr	6	
Capt Perry L Shuman	6	F4U ace
Maj Donald K Yost	6	
2Lt Thomas H Mann, Jr	5.5	+3.5 with VMF-224
Capt Robert M Baker	5	F4U ace
Maj Leonard K Davis	5	
2Lt Cecil J Doyle	5	KIA 7 November 1942
Capt Kenneth M Ford	5	F4U ace

Six pilots scored at least one victory with the unit en route to wartime totals of five or more – 1Lt O M Bate, 1Lt H H Long, 1Lt H A McCartney, Capt D C Owen, Maj R B Porter and Capt J H Reinburg. Porter and Reinburg also eventually gained commands of their own.

COLOUR PLATES

This 14-page section profiles many of the aircraft flown by the elite pilots of the US Navy and Marine Corps, plus the more notable Martlet naval aviators of the Fleet Air Arm. All the artwork has been specially commissioned for this volume, and profile artists Chris Davey, Keith Fretwell and John Weal, plus figure artist Mike Chappell, have gone to great pains to illustrate the aircraft and their pilots as accurately as possible following in-depth research. Aces' machines that have never previously been illustrated in colour are featured alongside accurate renditions of the more famous Wildcats from World War 2.

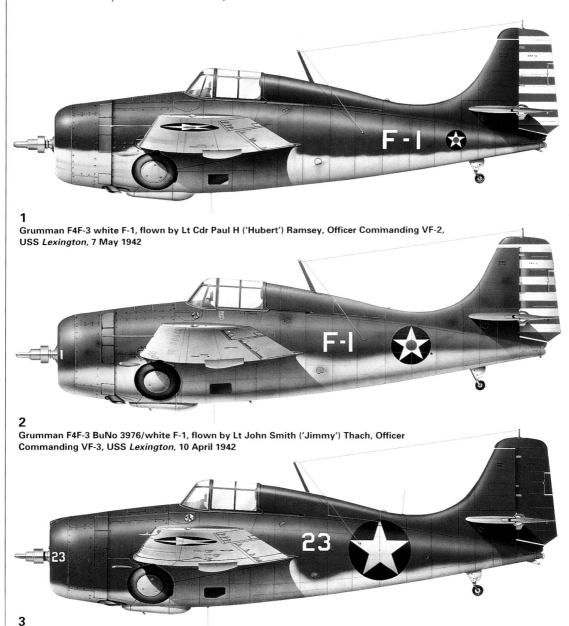

1
Grumman F4F-3 white F-1, flown by Lt Cdr Paul H ('Hubert') Ramsey, Officer Commanding VF-2, USS *Lexington*, 7 May 1942

2
Grumman F4F-3 BuNo 3976/white F-1, flown by Lt John Smith ('Jimmy') Thach, Officer Commanding VF-3, USS *Lexington*, 10 April 1942

3
Grumman F4F-4 BuNo 5093/white 23, flown by Lt Cdr John S Thach, Officer Commanding VF-3, USS *Yorktown*, Midway, 4 June 1942

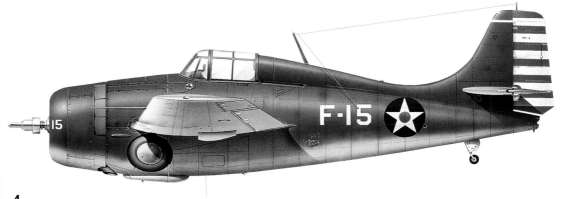

4
Grumman F4F-3 BuNo 4031/white F-15, flown by Lt Edward H ('Butch') O'Hare VF-3, USS *Lexington*, 20 February 1942

5
Grumman F4F-3 BuNo 3986/white F-13, flown by Lt Edward H O'Hare, VF-3, USS *Lexington*, 10 April 1942

6
Grumman F4F-4 BuNo 5192/black F12, flown by Lt James Julian ('Pug') Southerland, VF-5, USS *Saratoga*, 7 August 1942

7
Grumman F4F-3A BuNo 3916/white 6-F-5, flown by Ensign James G Daniels, VF-6, USS *Enterprise*, 7 December 1941

8
Grumman F4F-3A BuNo 3914/black F-14, flown by Lt Wilmer E ('Bill') Rawie, VF-6, USS *Enterprise*,
1 February 1942

9
Grumman F4F-4 BuNo 5075/black 20, flown by Machinist Donald Eugene Runyon, VF-6, USS
Enterprise, 24 August 1942

10
Grumman F4F-4 white 18, flown by AP/1c Howard Stanton Packard, VF-6, USS *Enterprise*,
August 1942

11
Grumman F4F-4 black 9-F-1, flown by Lt Cdr John Raby, VF-9, USS *Ranger*, *Operation Torch*, November 1942

12
Grumman F4F-4 BuNo 03417/white 19, flown by Lt Stanley Winfield ('Swede') Vejtasa, VF-10, USS *Enterprise*, 26 October 1942

13
Grumman F4F-4 BuNo 5238/white 14, flown by Ensign Edwin Lewis ('Whitey') Feightner, VF-10, USS *Enterprise*, 30 January 1943

14
Grumman F4F-4 white F21, flown by Lt(jg) William Nicholas Leonard, VF-11, Guadalcanal, June 1943

15
General Motors FM-2 white 17 of VF-26, USS *Santee*, October 1944

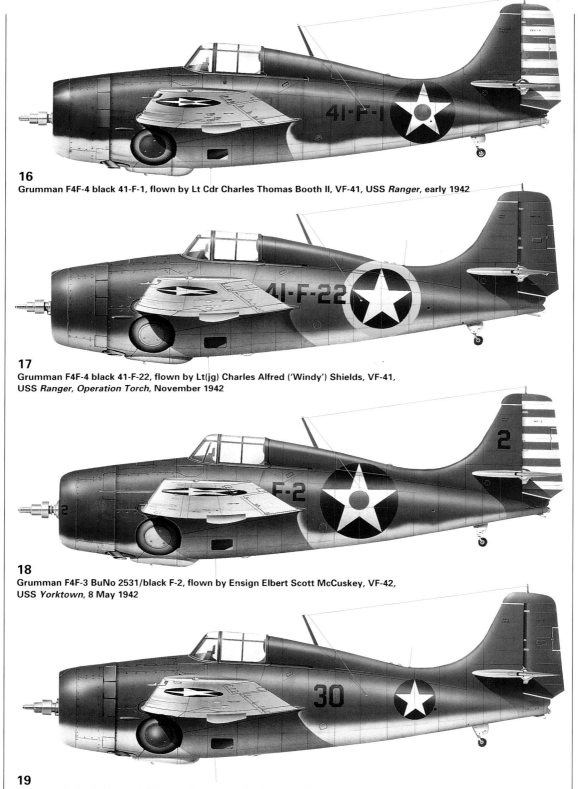

16
Grumman F4F-4 black 41-F-1, flown by Lt Cdr Charles Thomas Booth II, VF-41, USS *Ranger*, early 1942

17
Grumman F4F-4 black 41-F-22, flown by Lt(jg) Charles Alfred ('Windy') Shields, VF-41,
USS *Ranger*, *Operation Torch*, November 1942

18
Grumman F4F-3 BuNo 2531/black F-2, flown by Ensign Elbert Scott McCuskey, VF-42,
USS *Yorktown*, 8 May 1942

19
Grumman F4F-4 BuNo 02148/black 30, flown by Lt Cdr Courtney Shands, VF-71, USS *Wasp*, August 1942

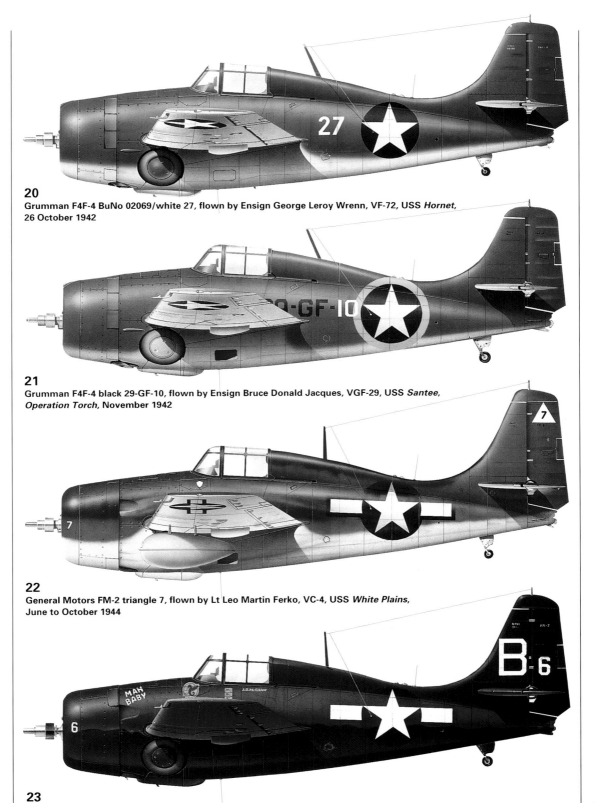

20
Grumman F4F-4 BuNo 02069/white 27, flown by Ensign George Leroy Wrenn, VF-72, USS *Hornet*,
26 October 1942

21
Grumman F4F-4 black 29-GF-10, flown by Ensign Bruce Donald Jacques, VGF-29, USS *Santee*,
Operation Torch, November 1942

22
General Motors FM-2 triangle 7, flown by Lt Leo Martin Ferko, VC-4, USS *White Plains*,
June to October 1944

23
General Motors FM-2 white B6 *MAH BABY*, flown by Ens Joseph D McGraw, VC-10, USS *Gambier Bay*, 24 October 1944

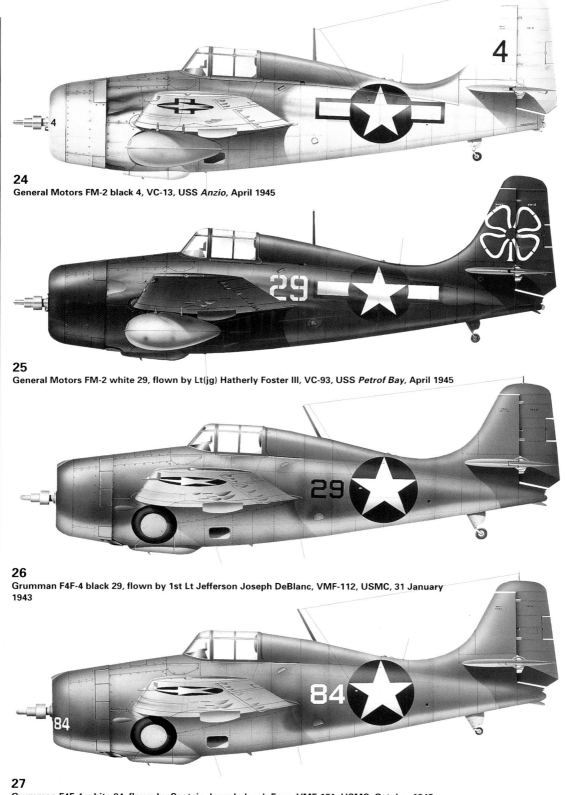

24
General Motors FM-2 black 4, VC-13, USS *Anzio*, April 1945

25
General Motors FM-2 white 29, flown by Lt(jg) Hatherly Foster III, VC-93, USS *Petrof Bay*, April 1945

26
Grumman F4F-4 black 29, flown by 1st Lt Jefferson Joseph DeBlanc, VMF-112, USMC, 31 January 1943

27
Grumman F4F-4 white 84, flown by Captain Joseph Jacob Foss, VMF-121, USMC, October 1942

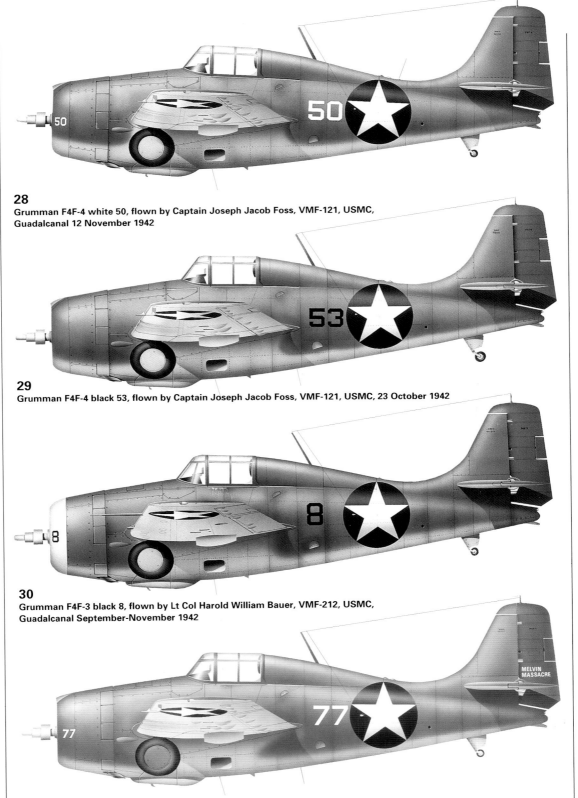

28
Grumman F4F-4 white 50, flown by Captain Joseph Jacob Foss, VMF-121, USMC,
Guadalcanal 12 November 1942

29
Grumman F4F-4 black 53, flown by Captain Joseph Jacob Foss, VMF-121, USMC, 23 October 1942

30
Grumman F4F-3 black 8, flown by Lt Col Harold William Bauer, VMF-212, USMC,
Guadalcanal September-November 1942

31
Grumman F4F-4 02124/white 77, flown by Lt James Elms Swett, VMF-221, USMC, 7 April 1943

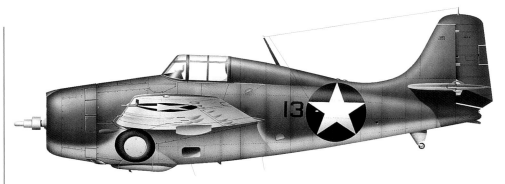

32
Grumman F4F-4 BuNo 02100/black 13, flown by Captain Marion E Carl, VMF-223,
USMC, Guadalcanal August 1942

33
Grumman F4F-4 BuNo 03508/black 13, flown by Captain Marion E Carl, VMF-223,
USMC, Guadalcanal September 1942

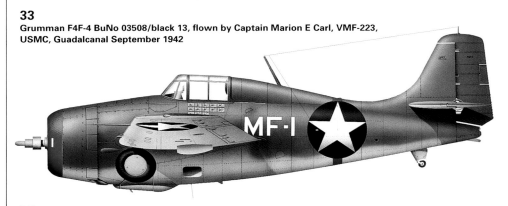

35
Grumman F4F-3 white MF-1, flown by Major R E Galer, VMF-224, USMC,
Guadalcanal September-October 1942

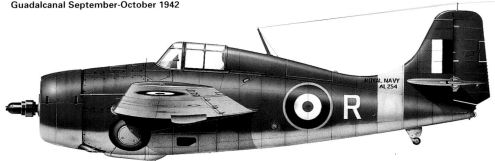

36
Grumman Martlet I AL254/R, flown by Sub-Lt Eric Brown, No 802 Sqn, Fleet Air Arm, HMS *Audacity*, 8 November 1941

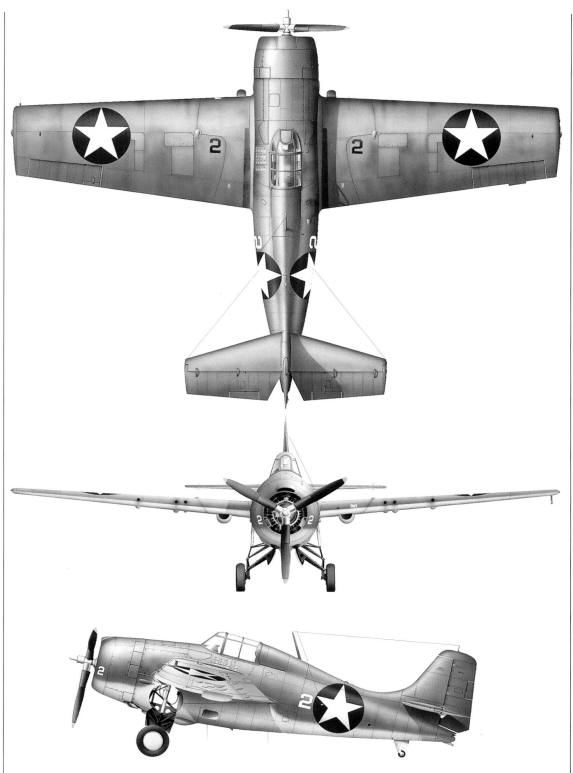

34
Grumman F4F-4 white 2, unit and pilot unknown, USMC, Guadalcanal September 1942

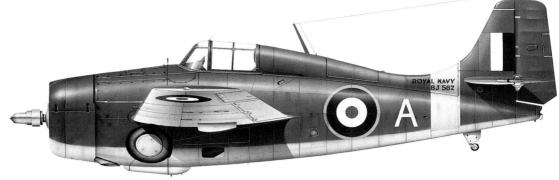

37
Grumman Martlet I BJ562/A, flown by Sub-Lt Parke, RNVR, No 804 Sqn, Fleet Air Arm, Skeabrae, Orkney,
24 December 1940

38
Grumman Martlet III AX733/K, flown by Sub-Lt W M Walsh RN, No 805 Sqn, Fleet Air Arm,
Western Desert, 28 September 1941

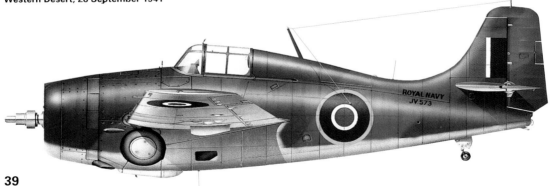

39
Grumman Wildcat V JV573, flown by Sub-Lt R A Fleischman-Allen RN, No 813 Sqn, Fleet Air Arm,
HMS *Vindex*, February 1945

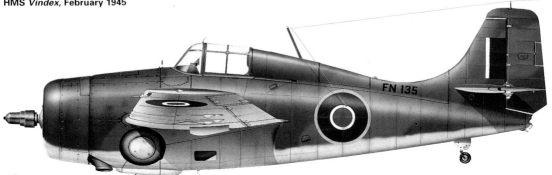

40
Grumman Wildcat (Martlet) IV FN135, Sub-Lt R K L Yeo RN, No 819 Sqn, Fleet Air Arm, HMS *Activity*, 30 March 1944

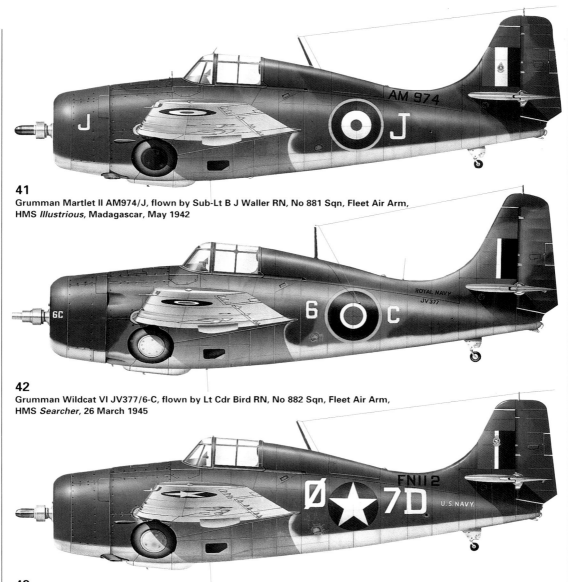

41
Grumman Martlet II AM974/J, flown by Sub-Lt B J Waller RN, No 881 Sqn, Fleet Air Arm,
HMS *Illustrious*, Madagascar, May 1942

42
Grumman Wildcat VI JV377/6-C, flown by Lt Cdr Bird RN, No 882 Sqn, Fleet Air Arm,
HMS *Searcher*, 26 March 1945

43
Grumman Martlet II FN112/0-7D, flown by Lt Dennis Mayvore Jeram RN, No 888 Sqn,
Fleet Air Arm, HMS *Formidable*, *Operation Torch*, 9 November 1942

1. Major Robert E Galer was CO of VMF-224 during its tour on Guadalcanal in late 1942

2. Leading ace at Guadalcanal was Captain Joe Foss of VMF-121. His flying attire is typical of the campaign

3. Martlet I pilot Sub-Lieutenant Eric 'Winkle' Brown of the Fleet Air Arm's No 802 Sqn in November 1941

4. Leading FM-2 ace Lieutenant Ralph Elliot was CO of VC-27 aboard USS *Savo Island* in 1944/45

5. Lieutenant of VF-21 in the Solomon Islands in late summer 1943

6. Lieutenant(jg) 'Butch' O'Hare of VF-3 in his green/grey service uniform in the New Year of 1942

ON THE OFFENSIVE

etween the convoy battle of mid-November 1942 and early February 1943, when the island was declared secure, the nature of the Guadalcanal campaign changed. In December 1942 four Marine Corps Wildcat squadrons were operating from the two fighter fields: VMF-112 (still under Maj Fontana), -121 (temporarily under 1st Lt W F Wilson), -122 (Capt E E Brackett) and VMO-251 (now under Maj J N Renner). In fact, by year-end VMO-251 pilots had claimed 11 more confirmed kills, the top scorers being 1st Lts M R Yunck and K J Kirk, Jr, with three each. Yunck finished the war an ace, adding two more victories while flying Corsairs over Okinawa in 1945.

Most of VMF-121's original pilots enjoyed leave in Australia over the Christmas period, returning to complete their combat tours in January. These included Capt Joe Foss, who ran his wartime total to 26 with three 'Rufe' floatplanes on 15 January. Ranging as far north as New Georgia, VMF-121 claimed 40 kills during the month, ending the most successful squadron tour in the 'Cactus Air Force'.

January ended with a flourish. On the 30th two divisions of VF-10 (now back aboard *Enterprise*) intercepted 12 'Betty' torpedo bombers intent on sinking the cruiser *Chicago* (CA-29). Already slowed by battle damage, she was vulnerable to attack near Rennell Island.

'The Big E's' lead division splashed three bombers, then 'Reaper Leader' himself – Jim Flatley – arrived. Only two 'Bettys' survived, but four lasted long enough to torpedo the crippled warship, which quickly capsized and sank. Ens E L Feightner, better known as 'Whitey', was credited with three kills in this, one of the last combats by carrier-based F4Fs. Like many other Wildcat pilots, he would become an ace in F6Fs during the Central Pacific offensive of 1944.

A land-based pilot got in plenty of shooting the next day. Newly-promoted 1st Lt Jefferson J DeBlanc of VMF-112 already had three confirmed kills when he led his division on an escort mission on 31 January. Covering bombers which attacked shipping at Vella Lavella, DeBlanc met a swarm of Japanese fighters at 14,000 ft. As the SBDs and TBFs withdrew, they were intercepted and called for help. Diving to 1000 ft, DeBlanc remained to fight, despite dwindling fuel, and in a low-level dogfight, claimed three 'Rufes' and two Zekes. 1st Lt J P Lynch and 2nd Lt J B Maas each destroyed a Zero as well. However, DeBlanc and Tech Sgt James Feliton were forced to bail out over Kolombangara Island. Both aviators were retrieved by the coastwatcher, who kept them away from the Japanese, before being rescued two weeks later. DeBlanc's successful fight against the odds would earn him a Medal of Honor.

During the first week of February, two old-line carrier squadrons made their last victory claims with F4Fs. Now based at New Caledonia, 'Fighting Six' splashed four patrol aircraft in three days to end the 'Shooting Stars' ' F4F combat. VF-72, flying from Guadalcanal, claimed six Zeros during strikes against New Georgia on the fourth. The old *Wasp* squadron then passed into history.

Medal of Honor winner 1st Lt Jefferson J DeBlanc was VMF-112 most successful pilot with eight kills. Five of these came on the last day of January when he led his division on a bomber escort mission against shipping at Vella Lavella. His charges were intercepted by a mixed formation of Zekes and 'Rufes', and he proceeded to shoot down two of the former and three of the latter, before he himself was forced to bail out. He then spent two weeks in hiding with coastwatcher forces, before being 'traded back' to the Marines for a sack of rice!

The 'Wolf Pack' of VMF-112 gather around their heavily decorated scoreboard in February 1943. Led by ace, Maj Paul J Fontana, this unit scored 61.5 kills during its tour at Henderson Field, which commenced in late October 1942. Three aces were produced by the squadron at 'Cactus' – the CO (5 kills, all of which were scored in 1942), 1st Lt J J DeBlanc (8 kills) and 1st Lt J G Percy (5 kills). This photograph was taken shortly before the squadron returned to the US, and shows 58 victories on the scoreboard

The same day that VF-72 closed out its combat log, another era opened in F4F history. A half-dozen escort fighting squadrons (VGF) were deployed in the Southwest Pacific early in 1943, but few of them flew from their parent carriers. *Sangamon* (CVE-26), *Suwannee* (CVE-27) and *Chenango* (CVE-28) largely operated their squadrons ashore, and nearly all the combat missions were flown from Solomons airfields.

Most successful of these was VF-21. Originally established as VGF-11, Lt Cdr C H Ostrom's squadron became VC-11 in March 1943, but was redesignated 'Fighting 21' soon after. Meanwhile, on 4 February Ostrom's Wildcats escorted two joint-service strikes on shipping at Munda. The day netted claims of 10 kills for three VGF-11 F4Fs.

The new order began to change in February, with the arrival of Maj W E Gise's VMF-124. As the first Corsair squadron in combat, 'Fighting 124' received much attention. Aside from superior performance, the F4U possessed greater range than the Wildcat, and immediately began fighter sweeps and escorts well up into the Solomons chain. Meanwhile, there was still ample work for F4Fs.

That work, however, was largely limited to the Marines. Few Navy fighters found combat from March through May, the exception being two scuffles by VF-27 and -28 around Cape Esperance and the Russells on 1 April. That deficit would soon be made up.

On 7 April the Japanese launched an awesome mission against Guadalcanal: 67 'Vals' under a cloud of 110 Zekes. They were intercepted by elements of three Marine and four Army squadrons flying F4Fs, F4Us, P-38s, -39s and -40s. Of the two F4F squadrons intercepting that afternoon, VMF-214 drew first blood. Capt George Britt's pilots claimed six Zeros and four Vals between Cape Esperance and Koli Point. Two were

This 'atmospheric' line-up shot was taken on 13 May 1943, during a month-long lull in the seemingly endless struggle to secure Guadalcanal. This temporary reprieve allowed both the Japanese to re-group for one final assault (which took place exactly a month from the date this shot was taken), and the USMC to begin phasing in the F4U Corsair in place of the Wildcat. The squadron featured in this view has previously been misidentified as VMF-223, who returned to the US after an exhaustive combat tour in late October 1942. These weary machines actually belong to VF-11 'Sundowners', who finished with 55 kills in-theatre, a score which made them the most successful Navy/Marine fighter squadron at Henderson Field in 1943. Note the pilots' salubrious 'tent city' erected in amongst the palms, which was easily within sprinting distance of the makeshift flightline
(via Aeroplane)

credited to Tech Sgt Alvin J Jensen, one of the last enlisted pilots flying fighters. Shortly commissioned a lieutenant, Jensen would finish the war with seven confirmed kills. It was the squadron's only combat in F4Fs.

Next up was VMF-221 under Capt Robert Burns. While the Zero escort tied up most interceptors, a running battle drifted eastward from Esperance toward the anchorages. By that time, F4Fs and Army fighters had cut nearly 30 Zekes out of the pack, but the 'Vals' remained nearly intact. Therefore, the Aichis went for US shipping off Tulagi, leaving only one Wildcat division to handle the bombers.

The VMF-221 division leader was 1st Lt J E 'Zeke' Swett, entering his first combat. As 15 'Vals' rolled into their dives from 15,000 ft, Swett tagged onto the hindmost and flamed two. Then, entering the US flak zone, he pressed home his attack and caught another as it pulled out above the water. However, his F4F was then struck by a US anti-aircraft shell. He circled briefly over a nearby island, assessing the damage, then rejoined the fight.

Spotting five Aichis retiring northward, Swett bent his throttle to overtake them. Again working from back to front, he splashed two in passes from low astern. That made five. He then overtook another string of 'Vals' a mile-and-a-half ahead. Conscious of his dwindling ammunition, he bored in close and triggered economical bursts; two more went down.

At that point Zeke Swett might have disengaged. Instead, he overhauled the last visible 'Val' and traded machine-gun fire with the rear gunner. Both scored hits. The 'Val' trailed off, dragging a smoky plume, while Swett ditched his battered Wildcat. After nearly drowning he was retrieved by a PT boat, and was destined to receive the Medal of Honor. Staff Sgt Jack Pittman also claimed a 'Val', the 12th credited that day. It exactly matched the Japanese recorded loss of Aichis. However, the enemy only admitted nine of the claimed 27 Zeros, compared to seven F4Fs lost (with all Wildcat pilots safe).

The 'Vals', largely unmolested, sank a tanker and two destroyers. Overall, American fighters were credited with 40 shootdowns versus 29 acknowledged in Japanese records. Only one Corsair pilot got a shot in, and though Army fighters claimed 11 Zeros, the major killing was done by F4Fs.

The events of 7 April marked the last Marine Corps combat involving Wildcats in the Solomons. By 19 May VMF-221 had converted to Corsairs, as did -214 in June. Later that summer whilst flying Corsairs, -214 would become better known as the 'Black Sheep'.

Guadalcanal and environs were reasonably quiet for the rest of April and most of May. June was another matter. On the 12th VF-11's Lt W N Leonard intercepted more than 30 Zeros 10 miles northwest of Russell Island. Though low on fuel, the 16 'Sundowners' piled in and emerged with 14 kills. Five went to Lt(jg) Vernon E Graham, who became the Navy's only land-based ace in a day, and the last to 'turn the trick' in a Wildcat. Out of fuel, he crashed attempting a dead-stick landing, but recovered to fly again. Marine F4Us claimed six more victories.

Japan's displaced carrier air groups again struck Guadalcanal on the 16th. The attack involved 94 aircraft, the biggest raid since 7 April. It was also a big day for the defenders, 'AirSols' fighters claiming 76 kills from the 94 attackers. Forty-two were credited to Army fliers, including five Zeros by P-38 pilot 1st Lt Murray J Shubin. But again the top squadron was VF-11, led by the CO, Lt Cdr Charles M White. Several 'Sundowners' got among the bombers, with Lt(jg)s Charles R Stimpson and James S Swope claiming four and three, respectively. Six US fighters were lost, including three F4Fs and a P-40 in collisions. The Corsairs only managed fleeting shots at three Zeros.

Another full day of battle occurred on 30 June. Covering the Rendova landings, adjoining New Georgia, US fighters claimed 112 shootdowns – 67 by Corsairs, 34 by the Navy and 11 floatplanes picked off by Army fighters. It was an all-day event, lasting from mid-morning into late afternoon, ranging all over the Munda area. Controlled by ship-based fighter directors, VF-21 had 32 Wildcats airborne on dawn CAP, orbiting with drop tanks nearly 200 miles from Guadalcanal. Lt Cdr Ostrom's pilots anticipated plenty of shooting, and they were not disappointed. During the day they claimed 32 victories against four losses. Lt(jg) W C Smith tagged two Zeros and a 'Betty', as did Lt(jg) G F Boyle. Lt Ross Torkelson got two 'Bettys' and a probable,

In 1943 the highest scoring F4F fighter units in the US Navy were shore-based, VF-21 and -11 sharing over 120 kills in an eight-month period. One of the latter unit's most successful pilots at this time was Lt(jg) Vernon E Graham, who became the sole land-based naval 'ace in a day' when he destroyed five A6Ms on 12 June out of a force of 30 intercepted by 16 VF-11 F4F-4s northwest of the Russell Islands. The unit claimed a further nine Zeros, and despite returning to 'Cactus' without fuel, Graham still managed a dead-stick crash landing

This 'Sundowners' ' F4F-4 Wildcat sustained battle damage in July 1943, near the end of the squadron's tour. The aircraft displays typical markings of the period – two-tone blue/grey basic scheme with four-position stars. White stenciled 'F27' on the fuselage and '27' on the wings and cowing are augmented by VF-11's distinctive 'Sundowner' insignia below the windscreen *(via Robert L Lawson)*

while two other future aces, John Symmes and Tom Roach, both scored doubles.

The Rendova landing presented F4F pilots with their last major combat of the war. By August all South Pacific Marine fighter squadrons had re-equipped with F4Us, and the little Grumman's tenure finally expired. That same month the last Navy squadrons flying F4Fs in the Southwest Pacific were withdrawn from combat: VF-26, -27 and -28, based in the Russells. Each listed 10 to 12 victories in the April to July period. The last recorded kills by Navy F4Fs in the Pacific occurred on 25 July when VF-21 claimed eight Zekes near Munda. Ens N W Hutchings got three while Lt(jg) T H Moore splashed two. When the smoke finally cleared, an era in US naval aviation had ended.

SOLOMONS SUMMARY

From February through to July, VF-21 (by whatever designation) claimed 69 aerial victories – tops for 1943 F4F squadrons. In fact, VF-21 was surpassed only by the Corsairs of VMF-213 as the top 'AirSols' fighter squadron in the period ending in August, when F4Fs finally disappeared from combat. During the first eight months of 1943, F4Fs still claimed 44 per cent of all aerial victories credited to Navy and Marine fighting squadrons in the Pacific Theatre.

Overall, 'Cactus' and carrier-based F4F squadrons produced about 30 aces by the time the Japanese evacuated in early February 1943. Another five Navy and four Marine aces had emerged from Guadalcanal and environs by that summer, when the air war moved toward Rabaul. All were land-based aviators, who helped 'use up' the remaining Navy F4F-4s in the theatre.

Two VF-11 'Sundowners' made the list, Lt(jg)s Charles R Stimpson and Vernon E Graham claiming six and five kills respectively, while James S Swope came painfully close with 4.67 (Stimpson and Swope both became Hellcat aces during 1944). 'Fighting 21' produced three aces in 1943: Lt Ross E Torkelson, killed on 22 July, plus Lt(jg)s John Symmes and Thomas D Roach. Lt(jg) Cecil E Harris of VF-27 opened his victory log in the Solomons before going on to greater success with *Intrepid*'s (CV-11) VF-18 in late 1944. Another future ace who scored his first success in VF-27 F4Fs was Lt Sam L Silber who, as a lieutenant commander, led Hellcats from *Bunker Hill* (CV-17) during VF-18's 1943-44 deployment.

Among the top Marines, Smith, Bauer, Galer and Foss received the Medal of Honor (MoH) for their 1942 combat, as did Lts Jeff DeBlanc of VMF-112 and Jim Swett of -221 for their exploits early in the New Year. In all, seven F4F pilots received their nation's highest

While the Solomons campaign progressed into early 1943, new F4F squadrons were engaged in training in the United States. Here, six Wildcats of VF-24 slide into echelon over Floyd Bennett Field, New York, during April. The squadron eventually deployed with the far more capable F6F-3 Hellcats in the light carrier *Belleau Wood* (via Robert L Lawson)

decoration, including Capt Elrod of Wake Island and Lt(jg) O'Hare of the Navy – nearly half of all MoH fighter pilots in the Pacific War.

However, that conflict was not quite over for the Wildcat. As part of the Fourth Wing in the Ellice Islands, 1100 nautical miles east of Guadalcanal, VMF-111 and -441 were the last Marine combat squadrons flying Wildcats. Though the war along the International Dateline was tedious by Solomons standards, it could turn violent on occasion. VMF-441 had the distinction of scoring the last F4F victories in US service: two bombers were destroyed and one damaged by Capt W P Boland, Jr, during raids against Funafuti on 27 March and 8 August 1943. However, -441 received some FM-1s in December and began converting to Corsairs in January 1944. After that, the only Marine Corps Wildcats remaining in the Pacific Theatre were a few F4F-4 'hacks' and photo F4F-7s attached to headquarters and service squadrons.

The class of 1943

Combat from January to July 1943 produced the last F4F aces, which are listed as follows:

1Lt J E Swett	VMF-221	7	+8.5*
Lt(jg) C R Stimpson	VF-11	6	+10*
Lt R E Torkelson (KIA)	VF-21	6	
Lt(jg) T D Roach	VF-21	5.5	
Lt(jg) J C C Symmes	VF-21	5.5	+5.5*
1Lt J J DeBlanc	VMF-112	5	+3[†]
Lt(jg) V E Graham	VF-11	5	
Capt F E Pierce, Jr	VMF-121	5	+1[†]
1Lt J G Percy	VMF-112	5	+1[†]

Note – † indicates prior F4F victories in 1942
* indicates later victories in F4Us or F6Fs

Pacific F4F Squadron Scores (from January to August 1943)

VF-21	69	Solomons (includes 10 kills as VGF-11)
VF-11	55	Guadalcanal
VMF-121	40	Guadalcanal
VMF-112	25	Guadalcanal
VMF-221	25	Guadalcanal
VMO-251	20	Guadalcanal
VF-10	13	*Enterprise* and Guadalcanal
VF-27	12	Solomons and Russells
VF-28	12	Solomons and Russells
VF-26	11	Solomons and Russells
VMF-214	10	Guadalcanal
VF-72	6	Guadalcanal
VF-6	4	New Hebrides
VMF-441	2	Ellis Islands
Total	**304***	

*F4U score during the same period was 386

TORCH AND *LEADER*

I n comparison to the Pacific war, the F4F's contribution to the European Theatre was almost minuscule. Aside from anti-submarine composite squadrons embarked in escort carriers (CVEs), US Navy Wildcats participated in only two significant actions against the European Axis powers. The first of these was also the largest – Operation *Torch*, the invasion of French Morocco in November 1942.

Four American carriers were committed to *Torch* – *Ranger* and *Suwannee* (CVE-27) supporting the main landing force at Casablanca, with *Sangamon* (CVE-26) and *Santee* (CVE-29) off the northern and southern beaches, respectively. In all, they embarked some 109 F4F-4s, plus SBD-3s and TBF-1s.

Opposing the US landings were naval, air and land forces of the Vichy government of France. The prospect of combat against a traditional American ally – even one now aligned with Nazi Germany – seemed extremely ironic to many carrier pilots. And the irony only increased as one of the French units based in Morocco traced its genealogy to the *Escadrille Lafayette* of 1916.

US Army troops went ashore on 8 November against erratic opposition. However, the French Air Force put up a fight. During three days of almost constant flying, the largely-untried F4F pilots gave far better than they got from the more experienced French, who were mounted on Dewoitine 520s and Curtiss Hawk 75s. The major aerial combat occurred on 8 November when carrier pilots claimed 18 victories. Thirteen kills fell to Lt Cdr C T Booth's VF-41 in a dogfight north

of Cazes Airfield. The CO of their *Ranger* team-mates, VF-9's Lt Cdr John Raby, added one more. The remaining four were claimed by pilots of VGF-26 aboard the escort carrier *Sangamon*.

The second day's operation brought far less combat, with honours going exclusively to *Ranger* Wildcats. 'Fighting Nine' claimed five kills and VF-41 a solitary victory during missions around Fedala. The CVE-based units were in action again on the 10th as a VGF-29 pilot off *Santee* shot down a Potez 63 inland.

Throughout Operation *Torch*, 25 French air force and naval aircraft were claimed shot down by F4Fs, though two British machines were also probably destroyed in error. The top scores were as follows:

Lt(jg) C V August	VF-41	*Ranger*	2
Lt M M Furney	VF-41	*Ranger*	2
Lt(jg) B N Mayhew	VF-41	*Ranger*	2
Lt Cdr J Raby	VF-9	*Ranger*	2
Lt(jg) C A Shields	VF-41	*Ranger*	2
Lt E W Wood, Jr	VF-41	*Ranger*	2

Whilst its West Coast brethren were slugging it out over the vast Pacific battle front, F4F-4-equipped VF-41 on the East Coast were forced to bide their time flying mundane patrols over the mid-Atlantic from their parent carrier USS *Ranger*. BuNo 4084 exhibits all the standard markings worn by US Navy fighters in the first six months of the war. The squadron's chance of glory would eventually come at the end of 1942, however, when the Ranger Air Group flew support missions for the Allied *Torch* invasion force that landed in Vichy French territory in North Africa in November. By that stage all red in the national insignia had been deleted, with VF-41's Wildcats having had a thin yellow ring added to the edge of the roundel specially for this operation *(via Phil Jarrett)*

A VF-41 F4F-4 is waved on its way from *Ranger*'s wooden decks as a pair of US Army Piper L-4 Cubs cruise incongrously overhead – a handful of these spotter aircraft were ferried out to North Africa for the army aboard *Ranger*. To the right of the Wildcat is fresh ordnance for the ship's 18 SBD-3 Dauntlesses of VS-41, which were heavily involved attacking Vichy French naval and air force installations. *Ranger* boasted no less than 54 F4F-4s, split evenly between VF-9 and -41, going into *Torch*, but suffered considerable losses to enemy air and ground fire – 12 Wildcats destroyed in total, with four pilots killed and three cpatured. However, these losses were somewhat overshadowed by VGF-29's experience aboard the escort carrier USS *Santee* (CVE-29). In barely three days of combat, the unit lost no less than 10 of its 12 Wildcats. Four of these were written off in landing accidents at the short and muddy emergency airstrip at Safi – fortunately, only a single pilot, Lt(jg) G N Trumpter, was killed in amongst all this carnage, his F4F-4 crashing in the Atlantic due to a loss of oil pressure whilst on a dawn patrol with VGF-29 on the morning of the invasion. He was never found *(via Jerry Scutts)*

Despite their successes, overall US attrition was serious. By 11 November, in addition to five air-to-air losses, another six F4Fs had fallen to flak, and 14 more were lost operationally. The heaviest burden was carried by *Ranger*'s two fighter squadrons, as VF-9 and -41 lost a dozen Wildcats between them. Still, *Torch* proved valuable to dozens of young fighter pilots who tested their tactics and their skills over Morocco before moving on to the Empire of Japan. One of Lt Cdr John Raby's VF-9 pilots was Ens Marvin J Franger, who shot down a Curtiss H-75 over Morocco. By war's end Franger was the only Navy ace with confirmed victories on each of his three combat tours, flying from the decks of four different carriers.

Atlantic F4F Squadron Scores in 1942-43

VF-41	14	*Ranger*	Operation *Torch*
VF-9	6	*Ranger*	Operation *Torch*
VGF-26	4	*Sangamon*	Operation *Torch*
VF-4	2	*Ranger*	Operation *Leader*
VGF-29	1	*Santee*	Operation *Torch*

Almost a year after *Torch* the British Home Fleet supported a strike against German shipping in Bodø, Norway. The muscle behind Operation *Leader* was *Ranger* with Air Group Four. Because the Pacific Theatre had priority for F6F-3 Hellcat production, VF-4 still flew F4F-4s. However, Lt Cdr Charles L Moore had no less than 27 Wildcats both for strike escort and Force CAP when *Ranger* launched her air group north of the Arctic Circle on 4 October 1943.

Two strikes were launched during the morning, both escorted by Wildcats. The F4Fs' primary role was flak suppression, as no German aircraft opposed the mission. Lt Cdr Moore's aircraft sustained hits, and though two SBDs and a TBF were lost, seven Axis-controlled ships were successfully sunk.

That afternoon the task force retired westward, still within range of

Adorned with the distinctive yellow-ringed national insignia applied specially for *Torch*, a small section of *Ranger*'s burgeoning Wildcat force lets fly with a 36-gun broadside of .50 cal ammunition. All 54 F4F-4s systematically had the 'cobwebs' blown out of their Brownings in the days leading up to the invasion, the weapons also being calibrated and aligned. Squadron armourers can be seen on the wings of each aircraft, checking that the belt-fed ammunition passes smoothly through the gun breeches. No doubt making an unheavenly din below decks, a fair proportion of the crew – including a handful of interested, and somewhat anxious, fighter pilots – have ventured out to watch the spectacle *(via Jerry Scutts)*

land-based aircraft. *Ranger's* fighter director controlled two divisions of F4Fs, and put Lt B N Mayhew's section onto a radar contact. Mayhew and Ens D S Laird made short work of the Junkers Ju 88 'snooper', which crashed 22 miles from the carrier. Minutes later a Heinkel He 115 got somewhat closer before falling afoul of Lt E F Craig's division, again including Mayhew and Laird – the floatplane splashed 13 miles from *Ranger*. One Wildcat crashed on landing and went over the side, but the pilot was saved.

This combat was the US Navy's first success against the Luftwaffe. Moreover, 'Diz' Laird, later credited with five Japanese aircraft, became the only Navy ace to score against both major Axis powers. The F4F's final air-to-air claim against Germany was a Dornier Do 217D bomber, damaged by a VC-6 aircraft off *Core* (CVE-13) nearly 500 miles west-southwest of Brest on 22 December.

By that time the Wildcat was well established in its primary role against Germany – supporting anti-submarine operations. In early 1943 the US Navy began to close the dreadful mid-Atlantic gap – the ' black hole' – wherein merchant convoys were beyond the range of land-based patrol aircraft. The 8300-ton *Bogue* (CVE-9) class carriers were based on merchant ship hulls, with 442 x 81-ft flight decks – tiny by any standard, but adequate to the challenge. Escort carriers operating composite squadrons of TBF-1 Avengers and F4F-4 Wildcats were specially trained in 'hunter-killer' tactics to locate and destroy U-boats. *Bogue*'s VC-9 scored the first

The pilot gently eases open the throttle of his F4F-4 in anticipation of the signal to launch midway through the opening day of hostilities on 8 November 1942. The aircraft is fitted with a pair of 58-gal drop tanks, which significantly improved the Wildcat's modest combat radius, without comprimising its exemplary 'deck manners'. This machine was part of the Ranger Air Group
(via Aerospace Publishing)

A year after its bitter baptism of fire over French Morocco, the redesignated VF-29 was still operating in the Atlantic aboard the cramped decks of Santee, although the enemy was now German U-boats. The unit's dozen F4F-4 had also adopted a distinctive three-tone colour scheme unique to this theatre by the time this shot was taken in November 1943. The 'Atlantic' scheme consisted of Non-Specular Dark Gull Grey upper surfaces, NS Insignia White fuselage sides and Gloss White under-surfaces. VF-29 eventually transferred to USS Cabot (CVL-28) in the Pacific in early 1944 after recieving FM-2s (via Jerry Scutts)

hunter-killer success on 22 May, their result being dramatically out of proportion with their numbers. By summer's end, the Battle of the Atlantic had swung in favour of the Allies.

It would be unfair to attribute conquest of the U-boats solely to CVEs, as other factors were significant. Increasing numbers, and effectiveness, of escort vessels, as well as signals intelligence, were important. But the hunter-killers produced disproportionate results merely by their presence. Nobody will ever know how many U-boat commanders had their attacks thwarted simply because carrier aircraft were airborne near a convoy.

Nor would it be accurate to assign major importance to the F4F's ASW role. Wildcats contributed by spotting U-boats and suppressing anti-aircraft fire from surfaced submarines, allowing Avengers to press for the kill. But not even six-gun fighters were immune from the volume of flak that U-boats could put up after Adm Doenitz promulgated his famous 'fight back' order of mid-1943.

German submarines sprouted a forest of AA guns – single- and multiple-mount 20 and 37 mm. And they were effective. Throughout the Battle of the Atlantic, U-boats shot down at least seven US Navy aircraft. The first occurred on 13 July 1943 when a Core search team found U-487 on the surface, 700 miles south of the Azores. Lt(jg) E H Steiger led the attack in his Wildcat, strafing ahead of Lt R P Williams' Avenger. The TBF straddled the submarine with four depth charges, then pulled off to evaluate the situation.

Calling for reinforcements, Williams needed to slow the submarine lest it escape. He requested another strafing run and, though the F4F had only one gun firing, Steiger attacked. But this time the AA gunners were fully alert, filling the sky with flak. The Wildcat nosed down and crashed near the U-boat. However, two more F4Fs and a pair of TBFs shortly arrived, led by VC-13's skipper, Lt Cdr C W Brewer. Four more depth charges finally put paid to U-487's brief, but bloody, career.

In February 1944 FM-2s began replacing F4F-4s and FM-1s in East Coast composite squadrons. By VE-Day the late-model Wildcats equipped all 13 East Coast VC units, which averaged nine FM-2s and a dozen TBM-1Cs or -1Ds.

At war's end the US hunter-killer groups had sunk 54 U-boats, including 30 by air action alone. The Battle of the Atlantic never generated the individual acclaim common to aerial combat in the Pacific, but the strategic effect proved incalculable.

THE EASTERN WILDCAT

In addition to the 54 aces in F4Fs, four other fighter pilots scored five or more victories in 'the wilder Wildcat'. The FM-2 flew from escort carriers throughout 1944 and 1945, supporting amphibious and anti-submarine operations. However, the versatile aircraft also served admirably in close air support, spotting naval gunfire, and – when the occasion arose – aerial combat.

Grumman stopped building Wildcats and Avengers in 1943 to concentrate on the F6F Hellcat. Therefore, the Eastern Aircraft Division of General Motors Corporation took up F4F and TBF production so both types could remain in fleet service. The FM-1 was merely an Eastern-built F4F-4, but the follow-on fighter was 'a cat of a different colour'.

The FM-2 actually began life as the XF4F-8. Powered by a Wright R-1820, and distinguished by its taller vertical stabiliser and rudder, the lighter, more powerful, Wildcat first flew in late 1942. After Eastern learned the methods of large-scale production, FM-2s began rolling off the Linden, New Jersey, assembly line in September 1943.

The organisation of most CVE units contrasted with their big-deck counterparts. Composite squadrons contained both bombers and fighters in a single command, typically with 12 FM-2s and nine or more TBM-3s. Generally, the squadron commander flew Avengers while a senior fighter pilot led the FM contingent. There were, however, a few CVE 'air groups' organised along the lines of *Independence*-class CVLs, with separate fighter and torpedo squadrons.

As deliveries increased, FM-2s began appearing in deployed squadrons early in 1944. The new fighter's first aerial victory probably occurred on 20 March 1944 while USS *Midway* (CVE-63) sailed north of New Ireland in the Bismarck Archipelago. In a brief scuffle Lt(jg) J H Dinneen and Ens R P Kirk of VC-63 claimed the destruction of a 'Tony', a Japanese Army fighter, for the squadron's only victory of the war.

The next score occurred a fortnight later during a task group operation near the Marianas. On 6 April Lt(jg) R N Glasgow of *Coral Sea*'s (CVE-57) VC-33 splashed a 'Betty' bomber off Saipan. This area became a major venue for Wildcat operations when, in mid-June, the Fifth Fleet approached the Marianas in force. During operations leading up to the invasion of Saipan, seven more composite units scored their first kills.

Eastern Aircraft Division of General Motors Corp began delivering FM-2s to the fleet in early 1944. Bearing the striking 'Atlantic' scheme, this Wildcat of Composite Squadron (VC) 13 was based on the escort carrier *Tripoli* in March of that year. Lighter, yet more powerful, than the F4F-4, the FM-2 redressed the performance disadvantage which the Grumman fighter had ceded to Japanese opponents for two years. However, aerial combat in the European Theatre was limited to a one-day strike launched from *Ranger* against Bodø, Norway, in October 1943. On that occasion VF-4 F4Fs shot down two German 'snooper' aircraft *(via Robert L Lawson)*

The most successful FM-2 unit was VC-27, which flew from *Savo Island* from late 1944 to early 1945. Credited with 62 aerial victories, the composite squadron produced five of the nine top-scoring FM pilots. This aircraft, BuNo 56805, bears the late-war gloss blue colour scheme, with *Savo Island*'s distinctive arrow emblem on the vertical stabilizer. Here, a rough arrested landing has resulted in a collapsed port landing gear on 10 January 1945, the squadron having commenced operations the previous day in support of an invading force landing in the Lingayen Gulf on the northern island of the Pilippines *(via Robert L Lawson)*

Perhaps the most widely-travelled Wildcat unit was VF-26. Flying F4Fs, the escort-carrier squadron participated in the North African invasion in November 1942 while flying from *Chenango*. Then, in early 1943, the escort carrier sailed to the Solomon Islands where VF-26 alternately operated from shipboard and ashore. After conversion to FM-2s, the squadron returned to combat aboard *Santee* from April to October 1944. In all, 'Fighting 26' claimed 46 victories during the war and produced one of only four FM aces: Lt Cdr Harold N Funk, who splashed six Japanese aircraft on 24 October during the Battle of Leyte Gulf *(via Robert L Lawson)*

The Battle of Leyte Gulf (or Second Philippine Sea) was a two-day 'slugfest' fought over 24-25 October 1944. Because the CVEs were so heavily engaged, it became the most intense period of aerial combat for FM-2s during the entire war. On the 24th carrier pilots were credited with 270 aerial victories, including 65 by 11 of the composite squadrons engaged. The most active were VC-3 and -27, each with 14 kills, and VF-26 with 11.

The last two Wildcat aces in a day were crowned on 24 October. Lt Kenneth G Hippe of VC-3 returned to *Kalinin Bay* (CVE-68) with a score of five 'Lillys' in 20 minutes, while other VC-3 pilots claimed nine more kills. Lt Cdr Harold N Funk flew two sorties from *Santee* (CVE-29), claiming four bombers and a Zeke in the morning, then an 'Irving' that evening – this was more than half of VF-26's total on the 24th.

Aerial combat abated the next day, with 37 FM-2 successes among the 71 total by naval aviators. However, it was an entirely different matter on the surface. At dawn on the 25th a large enemy force emerged from the eastern end of San Bernardino Strait between Leyte and Samar. Taken by surprise, and vastly outgunned, the CVE force of Rear Adm Clifton Sprague fought for its life.

Among the six carriers of 'Taffy Three' was *Gambier Bay* (CVE-73), embarking Composite Squadron 10. With almost no warning, pilots scrambled into their aircraft and frantically started engines as battleship and cruiser shells exploded close aboard. One of the FM-2 pilots was 20-year-old Ens Joseph D McGraw, who had three kills to his credit, including a pair of 'Lillys' from the day before. He recalls:

'I just beat my wingman, Leo Zeola, to the last fighter on the port

In October 1944 20-year-old Ens Joseph D McGraw downed three aircraft whilst with VC-10, then bagged two more as part of VC-80

VC-80 FM-2s in late 1944 display differing colour schemes. The lead Wildcat, number 11, wears the tri-colour pattern, while its wingman bears the late-war gloss blue overall. From October 1944 to January 1945 the squadron shot down 16 Japanese aircraft in the Philippine Islands: four 'Oscars', three 'Vals', two Zekes, two 'Tojos', and one 'Jake', 'Jill', 'Irving', 'Sally' and 'Tony'. Top scorer was Ens Charles Guthrie with 2.5 victories, closely followed by Lt J L Morrissey and Ens J D McGraw with two each. McGraw, displaced from VC-10 when *Gambier Bay* was sunk, became an ace as a result of victories with both squadrons *(via Robert L Lawson)*

side aft corner of the flight deck. In fact, it was my airplane, "Baker Six". I got it started and then had to wait for all the aircraft ahead of me to take-off, so I sat there counting shell splashes and getting in some quality prayer time!

'I got off as the last fighter, I think, as I had to dodge a big hole on the forward port corner of the deck just as Capt Viewig was throwing the ship into a turn. I seem to remember that the flight deck officer tried to get me to taxy all the way up to an area he had chosen as the proper take-off spot, but I poured on the coals, waved him out of the way and took off as soon as I saw the deck clear in front of me. That gave me a better chance to avoid the holes forward.'

Unlike many other displaced CVE pilots, McGraw avoided the crowded landing strip at Tacloban, on Samar, and sought a friendly flight deck. He landed aboard *Manila Bay* (CVE-61) and volunteered for a strike against retreating Japanese cruisers. His third flight of 25 October was a CAP, leading the second section in a VC-80 division. An accurate radar vector put the four Wildcats directly onto some 18 'Vals' and 12 Zekes. The ensuing combat illustrates the FM-2's ability against a well-flown A6M5 Zero. After flaming four 'Vals' in their first pass, the Wildcats pulled up to confront the top-cover Zekes. McGraw recalls:

'The leader of the Zeros was good and he hit our division leader in the engine, putting him in the water (he was later picked up). As I had pulled up so hard and steep, I lost my wingman, but avoided the Zeros as they dove by. So I rolled left out of my climb and saw the lead Zero and his wingman pulling up from downing our leader. I was in a great position above and to the right of his wingman, so I shot him in the engine and wingroot with a burst long enough to cause him to flame and explode.

'That either surprised or made the Zero lead really mad, because he did the tightest turn I've ever seen to try to get on me. But I also pulled up into a tight climbing left turn into him, and he missed his shot behind me. The FM-2's tight turn must have surprised him because I got around quickly on him into a head-on, and put a fast burst into his engine. That really made him mad, because he quickly pulled hard up into me in what I thought was an attempt to ram. I had also pulled up hard to avoid him; it was a close thing.

'As I looked over my shoulder, in another tight turn, I saw he was smoking heavily and already diving for the clouds. I also saw three more Zeros turning into me to cut me off from their smoking leader. I took a long-range shot at the nearest one as I turned and dove for the water, but only sieved his tail. Luckily I got away, enjoying the satisfaction of seeing them also turn back to where they had come from.

'The Zero leader was flying a dark-green aircraft with no white circles around the "red meatballs", and he had large white letters and numbers on his tail, with what looked like a white streak of light-

ning or slash marking across his tail below the letters and numbers. I had the feeling he was an old hand and had expected the old Wildcats to be easy prey, so he was surprised and let his temper get the better of him – he probably didn't know about the much-improved FM-2 version. I don't know what happened to him, but with his engine shot up I don't suppose he made it back to his base.'

Upon landing aboard *Manila Bay* after dark, McGraw had logged 11 hours in three missions. In all, VC-10 Wildcats scored eight victories during the day, including those initially claimed after having been displaced from their baby flat-top, which was sunk by enemy shellfire.

By far the most successful air-to-air composite squadron was VC-27. Between October 1944 and January 1945 *Savo Island*'s Wildcats splashed 61.5 enemy aircraft, including 17 bombers of various types. The CO, Lt Ralph Elliott, was credited with nine victories in that period – the highest score not only in FM-2s, but for all Navy Wildcat pilots. His VC-10 colleague, Joe McGraw, recalls Elliott as being 'a tough fighter pilot even before he got into combat'.

Another Wildcat ace was Lt(jg) George H Davidson, also of VC-27. He entered combat with VF-21 in the Solomons, scoring his first victory in 1943. However, he tallied three solo and three shared victories aboard *Savo Island* for a total of 4.5, and thus became the only 'composite' ace as a result of both F4F and FM service. Incredibly, three other VC-27 aviators each claimed 4.5 victories, giving *Savo Island* five of the top nine places among CVE fighter pilots.

VC-27 had 26 scoring fighter pilots within its total of 61.5 victories; a TBM gunner also scored a kill. The top five pilots claimed 27 shootdowns, or nearly half the total. Timing and opportunity proved decisive, as only four other CVE units (VF-26, VC-81 and -84, plus VOC-1) tallied 20 or more victories. VC-27's startling five-day performance in late October netted 28 shootdowns, followed by nine in mid-December and 24 more during four days in early January 1945.

During the Philippines, Iwo Jima and Okinawa campaigns, two FM-2 units provided crucial support as observation-composite squadrons. Specially trained to 'spot' naval gunfire, VOC-1 and -2 flew almost continuously during daylight, providing battleships and cruisers with accurate target information ashore. Flying from *Wake Island* (CVE-65) and

This Wildcat pilot collided with one of VC-80's TBM-1C Avengers upon landing aboard *Manila Bay*. CVEs were the smallest of all aircraft carriers, requiring precision flying even beyond that of the 'large' *Essex*-class ships. The flight deck of a *Casablanca*-class escort carrier measured 477 ft long, though the deck of an *Independence*-class CVL was two feet narrower. The fact that naval aviators routinely flew off these tiny ships in most weather, and often at night, speaks volumes for their highly-developed skills (*via Robert L Lawson*)

Ranking FM-2 ace Lt Ralph Elliot of VC-27 climbs aboard 'his' Wildcat, parked on the deck of *Savo Island* in late 1944. 'Baldy' was the name of his brother's German Shepherd!

Marcus Island (CVE-77), VOC-1 probably logged more hours per pilot than any other fighter squadron in the Pacific Fleet. The pilots also found opportunity for aerial combat, claiming 20 kills. Meanwhile, VOC-2 in *Fanshaw Bay* (CVE-70) splashed five bandits at Okinawa. But, undeniably, their greatest contribution was calling in gunfire for Marines fighting ashore.

One of the greatest coincidences in Naval Aviation history occurred on 12 January 1945. While TF-38 launched strikes against Japanese and Vichy French forces in Saigon and elsewhere, escort carriers maintained CAPs which turned up a few contacts. One of those was a 'Jake', intercepted about 350 nautical miles off the Indochina coast by two Wildcats off *Nehenta Bay* (CVE-74). The VC-11 section attacked and destroyed the floatplane – nothing unusual in that, except that the successful pilots were Lt(jg)s Alton S and Grant L Donnelly. It was the only occasion in US Navy history when two brothers shared an aerial victory. Furthermore, it was VC-11's only shootdown of the war!

By VJ-Day, FMs of 38 composite squadrons had been credited with some 432 aerial victories. The leading units were as follows:

The Top-Scoring FM-2 Squadrons

VC-27	*Savo Island*	61.5	+1 by TBM
VF-26	*Santee*	31	
VC-81	*Natoma Bay*	21	+1 by TBM
VOC-1	*Wake Island* and *Marcus Island*	20	
VC-84	*Makin Island*	19	+1 by TBM
VC-21	*Nassau* and *Marcus Island*	18	
VC-3	*Kalinin Bay*	17	
VC-75	*Ommaney Bay*	17	
VC-93	*Shamrock Bay*	17	
VC-5	*Kitkun Bay*	16	
VC-10	*Gambier Bay* and Tacloban Field	16	+1 by TBM
VC-80	*Manila Bay*	16	

Of the 432 aircraft shot down 12 per cent of the kills were claimed by nine pilots

The Top-Scoring FM-2 Pilots

Lt R E Elliott	VC-27	*Savo Island*	9
Lt Cdr H N Funk	VF-26	*Santee*	6 +.50
Lt K G Hippe	VC-3	*Kalinin Bay*	5
Ens J D McGraw	VC-10, -80	*Gambier Bay, Manila Bay*	5
Lt L M Ferko	VC-4, -20	*White Plains, Kadashan Bay*	5
Lt T S Sedaker	VC-84	*Makin Island*	4.83
Lt(jg) G H Davidson	VC-27	*Savo Island*	4.50 +1 in F4Fs
Ens T S Mackie	VC-27	*Savo Island*	4.50
Ens R E Pfeifer	VC-27	*Savo Island*	4.50

Although not photographed 50 years ago like the remaining aircraft in this volume, the Confederate Air Force's beautifully restored FM-2 is worthy of inclusion nonetheless as it wears authentic markings for little-publicised unit, VOC-1, who flew from the decks of USS *Wake Island* (CVE-65) and USS *Marcus Island* (CVE-77) in 1945. Heavily involved in the Iwo Jima and Okinawa invasions, this unit served as naval gunfire spotters, flying almost continually over the islands relaying information on the fall of shells back to the Navy's battleships and cruisers. Although fully occupied performing this specialised role, pilots from VOC-1 nevertheless managed to shoot down 20 Japanese aircraft, placing the unit fourth in the overall FM-2 kill rankings

Lt Kenneth G Hippe of VC-3 downed five 'Lily' bombers in a 20-minute spell on the first day of the Battle of Leyte Gulf (24 October 1944), thus becoming the last Wildcat 'ace in a day'. Lt Cdr Harold N Funk of VF-26 had also bagged five aircraft earlier that same morning, before going on to destroy a sixth latter in the day

FLEET AIR ARM

The Royal Navy's effect upon the F4F was considerable. The Fleet Air Arm (FAA) introduced the type to combat a year before Pearl Harbor, and exerted influence in its armament fit which ran contrary to opinion in US Navy squadrons. But for all that, the Wildcat was the first truly modern fighter flown from British carriers, and represented an enormous leap forward in Royal Naval aviation.

Until the verge of war in 1939, the Royal Air Force retained widespread control of naval aviation. Then, at nearly the last minute, the senior service recognised the importance of an integrated air component and moved to correct matters. The resulting 'dark blue versus light blue' arrangement was not wholly agreeable to all parties, as RAF Coastal Command retained control of maritime search and patrol. However, British carrier aviation was able to proceed apace, no longer fighting for RAF funds.

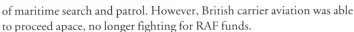

In September 1939, FAA strength was merely 231 aircraft, including 142 Swordfish and 46 Walrus. HMS *Glorious* embarked 12 Sea Gladiators, but clearly there was urgent need for a fast, modern, carrier fighter. Though navalised versions of the Hawker Hurricane and Supermarine Spitfire were eventually produced, neither was wholly satisfactory. The Seafire, especially, was susceptible to damage in ordinary deck landings, and the two-seat Fairey Fulmar – although built as a carrier fighter – lacked performance. Fulmars, which entered service with No 806 Sqn in September 1940, were followed by No 802's Martlets the next month. Some 25 kts faster than the Fulmar at sea level, the Grumman extended that advantage to 85 kts at altitude.

Ironically, France's *Aéronavale* became the source of Britain's original Wildcats. The G-36A export version was essentially an F4F-3 with Wright's R-1820 engine in place of the Pratt & Whitney. Eighty had been ordered but none could be delivered before France fell in June 1940. Consequently, the Royal Navy took over the original batch and soon ordered a further 100 G-36Bs with folding wings and the original R-1830 engines. These F4Fs were christened Martlet Mk Is and IIs, respectively.

Despite their advanced design, the Mk Is had limited utility. Hampered by French instrumentation, equipment and armament, they remained land-based with No 804 Sqn at Hatston. Difficulties with tailwheels and impromptu .50 cal mounts caused problems, but the Martlets served well enough. On Christmas Day 1940 a section from No 804 intercepted a Ju 88 reconnaissance bomber over the Home Fleet base at Scapa Flow. Lt L V Carter and Sub-Lt Parke shot out one engine, and the Junkers crash-landed in a bog near Loch Skail. The Martlet had drawn

One of the last survivors of the 85-strong batch of Martlet Is originally 'acquired' by the FAA is swung around into position on a recently defrosted ramp in Scotland in early 1942. Many of the ex-French G-36As had either been written off or retired from service by this stage, a handful lingering on with training squadrons around the UK. This weary example belonged to No 795 Sqn, one of several operational training units tasked with churning out qualified Martlet pilots. The more numerous Martlet Mk II was the favoured instructional tool by this stage in the war, although a handful of rare, fixed-wing, Mk IIIs (ex-Greek Navy) were also employed in tuitional roles
(via Aeroplane)

A trio of fixed-wing Martlet Is formate for the camera during an official photo-shoot staged for a Navy photographer in September 1941. One machine wears an individual letter code, whilst the lead fighter has the number '57' painted behind the roundel. A pale blue European theatre band has been applied at the base of the fin on each Martlet, this marking being more commonly seen on RAF fighters – FAA machines wore it for a very brief period in 1941/42 only. Although no distinguishing unit markings are visible, it is likely that these machines belong to either No 778 or 795 Sqns, both of which provided Martlet training at the time *(via Aeroplane)*

When this photo was released in September 1941, it was captioned, 'A Yankee fighter in the Royal Navy'! Now flying line abreast, the trio of Martlets featured in the previous shot hold an impeccable formation for the camera, which leads one to assume that these fighters aren't being flown by student pilots! *(via Phil Jarrett)*

first blood – that same month VF-4 accepted the US Navy's first F4F-3s.

The first Martlet squadron to make a carrier deployment was Lt Cdr John Wintour's No 802. Armed with six Mk IIs, the tiny unit boarded HMS *Empire Audacity* in September 1941, bound for the North Atlantic convoy routes to Gibraltar. *Audacity* was a captured German steamer – the 5500-ton *Hannover* – and although capable of only 14 kts, her quick conversion to an escort carrier over-rode her limited operational capability.

Wintour's Martlets were primarily intended to defend slow convoys from scouting and attack by long-range Luftwaffe bombers. However, the Grummans also proved useful in anti-submarine work by providing advance warning of enemy vessels. Two sightings were made during the first week out, forcing the U-boats to submerge. Then, on 21 September, Sub-Lts N H Patterson and G R P Fletcher got their chance. They bounced a Focke-Wulf Fw 200 Kondor which was bombing some torpedoed ships and, between them, fired 320 rounds of .50 cal to shoot off the aircraft's tail – interestingly, they identified it as a Kurier, the civil airliner from which the bomber had originated. That afternoon another Martlet section chased away a Ju 88 snooper. No 802 Sqn had been proven effective, but the outbound leg cost Convoy OG-74 five ships. The return to Britain in October met little opposition.

However, *Audacity* was back at sea before month's end, fighting worsening weather more than the Germans. High winds and heaving seas rendered flight operations difficult to impossible, with the CVE's deck pitching as much as 65 ft. One Martlet was lost overboard during the storms whilst attempting to land, but the pilot was recovered.

On 8 November Lt Cdr Wintour was vectored onto a radar contact, resulting in an interception. The CO made two passes, setting the Focke-Wulf alight, although it maintained level flight. However, one of the gunners got a clear shot at the Martlet and sent the Grumman down, before Sub-Lt Hutchinson finished off the Kondor. Later that day Sub-Lt Eric Brown's 'Red Section' flushed two Kondors and pursued them independently. 'Winkle' Brown fought a prolonged duel in heavy clouds, finally ending up nose-to-nose with the Fw 200. He splashed the bomber, but morale suffered – two shootdowns for loss of the popular CO was considered a poor exchange.

However, by now *Audacity* was proving her worth. Convoy OG-76 reached Gibraltar completely intact – a rare achievement in late 1941. No 802 did a quick turnaround in Britain and, under Lt Cdr Donald Gibson, returned to sea with only four Martlets to escort 32 merchantmen in mid-December.

The cruise began poorly and only worsened. On only the third day out Sub-Lt Fletcher attacked a surfaced U-boat which, rather than dive, chose to fight. Accurate 37 mm fire struck the Martlet, which crashed near *U-131*. Escorts finally sank the submarine that had killed Fletcher.

Two days later, on 19 December, 'Red Section' was again engaged. Eric Brown repeated his head-on tactics with similar results as before, becoming the first fighter pilot to destroy two Kondors. His wingman damaged another which escaped into cloud cover. That afternoon Lt Cdr James Sleigh's 'Yellow Section' found another bomber and he duplicated Brown's approach. Firing down to minimum range, he pulled up at the last second and just collided with the Fw 200. Back on deck he found part of the bomber's aileron lodged in his tailwheel.

The three remaining fighters were airborne almost constantly during daylight, reporting multiple contacts. But there was no aerial protection at night, the favoured hunting time of U-boat skippers. On the night of the 20th/21st *U-751* accomplished Adm Doenitz's orders to sink the troublesome carrier, a task it duly performed with three torpedoes. Loss of life was heavy, and only five pilots survived.

During its three-month combat career No 802 Sqn had shown the way to the future. By destroying five Fw 200s and diverting at least ten U-boats from their mission, the Martlets had proven the worth of escort-carrier fighters. More squadrons and more CVEs would follow.

During the period of *Audacity*'s North Atlantic convoys, another Martlet squadron was making itself known in warmer climes. No 805, previously of HMS *Formidable*, operated under RAF control at Sidi Haneish, Egypt, with eight Martlet IIIs (ex-Greek Navy F4F-3As diverted to the RN). Following inconclusive combats with Bf 109s and Me 110s, the unit finally scored on 28 September 1941. Flying a coastal patrol along the Libyan border, Sub-Lt W M Walsh engaged three Italian Fiat G.50s and emerged with the first Martlet victory over the second major Axis power in Europe.

Moving to Tobruk, No 805 found more combat along the coastal convoy routes. Sub-Lt A R Griffin broke up a *Regia Aeronautica* torpedo attack on 28 December, shooting down one SM.79 and dispersing the others. However, one of the Italian gunners had the range and shot the Martlet into the water. By July 1942 the squadron had accounted for two more Savoias and a Ju 88, then moved to East Africa for patrols over the Indian Ocean.

Carrier-based Martlets were also active in the region. Embarked in HMS *Illustrious*, Nos 881 and 882 Sqns participated in the occupation of Diego Suarez, Madagascar, in May 1942. From the 5th to the 7th the Mk IIs provided ground support and protected the task force

The Martlet II boasted two extra .50 cal Brownings and, most importantly, folding wings, as shown here in this superb Charles E Brown photograph. Like the Martlet I, it was built in small numbers, only 100 being delivered to the FAA from October 1940 onwards – the first ten Mk IIs were fitted with the old fixed wing, and were immediately relegated to training duties once in the UK. Of the remaining 90 aircraft, 36 were shared amongst a handful of squadrons operating from Home Fleet carriers, this particular machine belonging to No 881 Sqn aboard HMS *Illustrious*, for example. Along with sister-squadron No 882, this unit first saw action during the British occupation of the Vichy French naval base at Diego Suarez, on the island of Madagascar, in May 1942. Both strafing and combat patrols were flown by the units, although No 881 was the only squadron to shoot down enemy aircraft – two Potez 63-11 light bombers and a three Morane MS.406 fighters. In return, a single Martlet was shot down by the Vichy pilots. The FAA's highest scoring Martlet pilot of the war, Lt C C Tomkinson, claimed all 2.5 of his kills during this operation
(via Phil Jarrett)

from Vichy French aircraft. During that time No 881 shot down three MS.406 fighters and two Potez 63 fast reconnaissance bombers, in exchange for one Martlet that crash-landed. That left only one Axis enemy not yet represented among victims of the FAA's Grummans – an oversight about to be redressed.

Sailing the Bay of Bengal in early August, *Illustrious* and *Formidable* drew the attention of Japanese maritime patrols. On the 7th the British force was sighted by two Kawanishi H6K flying boats, one of which eluded interception. However, Sub-Lts J E Scott and C Ballard of 'Triple Eight' Squadron destroyed the second 'Mavis', rounding out an Axis grand slam for the Martlet.

Later that same month, Martlets were concerned with German and Italian opponents in the Mediterranean. Operation *Pedestal* involved three carriers – *Eagle, Victorious* and *Indomitable* – escorting a Malta-bound convoy with No 806 Sqn embarked in the latter. Though the bulk of the air defense was handled by 48 Sea Hurricanes and Fulmars, 806's half-dozen Grummans were heavily involved during repeated air raids on the 12th. Upwards of 100 bomber and torpedo aircraft were engaged, with Martlets accounting for four of the 30 claimed kills – two SM.79s, a Reggianne Re.2000 and a Ju 88. One Martlet was lost, as were a dozen other British fighters. Nor was such damage limited to FAA aircraft. By the time *Pedestal* was completed, *Eagle* had succumbed to a U-boat and only five of the 14 merchantmen reached Malta. However, these sacrifices were enough to sustain the island until the aerial siege finally ended.

The year's combat ended off Algeria during Operation *Torch* in November. Aside from the US Navy phase against French Morocco, two Royal Navy carriers with Martlets supported the eastern part of the plan. *Formidable*, now returned from the Indian Ocean, embarked No 888 and 893 Sqns with Mk IIs and IVs, respectively. No 882 Sqn aboard *Victorious* also flew Mk IVs, bringing the Grumman total aboard both ships to 42. The newer mark was, in fact, the F4F-4B, with the six-gun armament favoured by the Royal Navy.

Combat began on 6 November when Lt D M Jeram led a 'Triple Eight' section in chasing down a Bloch 174. Two days later a flight of No 882 Sqn 'captured' Blida Airfield near Algiers. This unprecedented accomplishment was consumated when the flight leader landed after observing white flags on the ground. While his wingmen circled overhead, Lt B H C Nation received the surrender of the pro-Allied base commander. After turning over his prize to

Vichy French forces swept from the sky, a No 881 Sqn Martlet II is manhandled back to its spot on *Illustrious*' salty deck following a patrol on 7 May 1942. Note the aircraft's wheel-chocks perched atop the port wing *(via Aeroplane)*

'Don't forget to put this on, sir!' By January 1943 No 882 Sqn had re-equipped with the ultimate Grumman Martlet, the Mk IV, and had switched carriers to HMS *Victorious (via Aeroplane)*

A considerable chunk of No 893 Sqn is spotted along the centreline of HMS *Formidable* prior to launching on patrol over the Mediterranean in February 1943. A sailor is positioned at each wing tip to prevent the Martlets from 'dinging' their flying surfaces when the carrier heels over into wind. Further crewmen await the signal below the fuselages that will see them whip the wheel chocks away. No 893 Sqn's next period of combat occured in July 1943 when they supported Operation *Husky*, which saw the Italian island of Sicily invaded by the Allies **(via Aeroplane)**

Illustrating just how 'mushy' the Martlet/Wildcat undercarriage really was, a No 878 Sqn Mk IV lists to port as the starboard wing is elevated by the stiff breeze blowing over *Illustrious*' bows. The pilot is gingerly taxying forward under the direction of the sailor in sandals(!), and once in position he will open the throttle and start his take-off run when he sees lieutenant(flying) drop his flag. This shot was taken in early 1944 whilst the carrier was sailing in the Mediterranean **(via Aeroplane)**

startled American troops, Nation returned to *Formidable* with a story to dine out on for a very long time!

The tentative Anglo-Franco truce was shattered on the 9th as Luftwaffe bombers interceded. Consequently, No 882 Sqn claimed a He 111 destroyed and a Ju 88 damaged, while No 888's Jeram bagged another Junkers, which he shared with his wingman.

Thus far in *Torch* the only Martlet squadron deprived of air combat was *Formidable*'s No 893. However, on the 11th a four-plane flight intercepted and shotdown a twin-engined aircraft identified as an Italian SM.84. Tragedy ensued when the FAA pilots later learned that they had actually destroyed an RAF Hudson based at Gibraltar.

The first half of 1943 was relatively uneventful for Martlet pilots. *Furious*' two fighter squadrons, Nos 881 and 890, plied the North Sea on generally fruitless patrols, but did turn up occasional business. Three Bv 138s were shot down during July before the venue shifted back to the Atlantic. The tri-motor Blohm und Voss seaplane would become the Martlet's most frequent victim, with 12 entries in the victory log.

At this same time in the Pacific, US Wildcats and British Martlets were co-mingling in the same ship. USS *Saratoga* and HMS *Victorious* had arranged a cross-deck evolution for a short period, combining all the fighters of both air groups in the latter carrier. There was some maintenance adjustment to be made, as Nos 882, 896 and 898 Sqns' Martlet IVs had Wright engines compared to the F4F-4's Pratt & Whitneys.

However, the Anglo-American force co-operated during Operation *Toenail* – seizure of New Georgia Island during late June and early July. 'Fighting Three', under Lt Cdr L H Bauer, experienced no problems operating with the FAA, despite different landing-signal procedures. In fact, the Americans rather favoured the arrangement, as they benefited from the Royal Navy custom of serving liquor aboard ship. At least one exuberant F4F-4 pilot reminded his shipmates of that fact by dropping a message on 'Sara's' flightdeck in a beer can – an *empty* beer can! *Victorious* departed the Pacific in August without having engaged Japanese aircraft.

On 1 December 1943 – two years after *Audacity's* loss – another Fw 200 fell afoul of Martlets. The escort carrier *Fencer* flew a composite squadron, No 842, consisting of Martlet Mk IVs and Swordfish, and two fighters tackled the lone Fw 200 with expected results. It was the sixth destroyed by British Martlets.

A new variant began arriving in late 1943 as Eastern FM-1s were delivered as Martlet Mk Vs. The

first combat for the new model occurred on 12 February 1944 when *Pursuer* launched elements of Nos 881 and 896 Sqns to defend against four-engined bomber attack. Armed with radio-controlled glide bombs, Fw 200s and He 177s tried to disrupt a Gibraltar convoy, but were intercepted by four Mk Vs. In a rare nocturnal combat, Martlets claimed one of each without loss. The carrier pilots reported that German gunners seemed to use the Martlet's glowing exhaust stubs as aiming points.

Four days later, and nearly 200 miles west of Ireland, *Biter's* Mk IVs claimed a Ju 290, adding yet another multi-engine bomber to the Grumman's growing list. Two New Zealanders, Lt W C Dimes and E S Erickson, fired 1460 rounds into the huge aircraft to ensure its destruction. However, the Junkers was the last victim of the Martlet. In March British names for American aircraft were standardised along US lines, so Royal Navy F4F and FMs also became Wildcats. So too did the Tarpon become the Avenger in British service.

Though Grumman fighters had long flown the appalling Arctic convoy routes, as yet they had found no conclusive combats. All that changed during March and April 1944. *Activity* and *Tracker*, with Nos 819 and 846 Sqns, escorted convoy JW-58, which was subjected to a near-constant enemy presence. Between 30 March and 1 April the Wildcat Mk IVs claimed six bombers, including three Kondors on the 31st – this raised the tally to ten Fw 200s destroyed by Martlets since September 1941.

Meanwhile, Operation *Tungsten* went ahead on 3 April as six Royal Navy carriers attacked the German battleship *Tirpitz* in a Norwegian fjord. CVEs *Pursuer* and *Searcher* contributed Wildcat Mk Vs, but no aerial opposition developed.

No 819 continued on its winning ways on 1 May while flying in

Not all Wildcat squadrons enjoyed the luxury of a large flight deck from which to operate, Nos 882 and 898 Sqns, for example, calling the modest confines of HMS *Searcher* home. This flypast was performed specially for photographer Charles E Brown in mid-April 1944, the carrier and her air wing having just come off of flak suppression missions flown in support of FAA aircraft attacking the pocket battleship *Tirpitz* in the Norwegian fjords *(via Aeroplane)*

Caught in mid-air by its 'sting' hook, a No 898 Sqn Wildcat IV comes back aboard *Searcher* to complete another successful strafing mission against German flak batteries in Norway *(via Aeroplane)*

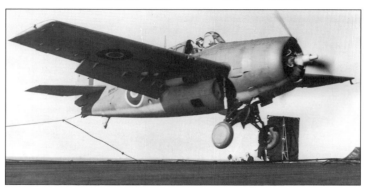

northern climes. 'Yellow Section' surprised a Bv 138 which had been stalking one of *Activity*'s Swordfish and splashed the snooper 26 minutes after launch. Lt Large and Sub-Lt Yeo credited the 'Stringbag' crew with radioing the enemy's position during the hunt. Nos 898 and 896 added three more Bv 138s in May and June.

Pursuer and *Searcher* appeared off Southern France in August with Nos 881 and 882 Sqns flying Mk VIs and Mk Vs, respectively. Operation *Anvil-Dragoon* thus marked the first major appearance of FM-2s in British service, but the Grummans were limited to strike missions and ground support. During the next three months, more Wildcats were involved in similar operations in the Aegean Sea – again without opportunity for air-to-air combat.

Attention shifted to the far north as *Campania* escorted a two-ship convoy, JW-61A. On 3 November No 813 Sqn's Lt Leamon and Sub-Lt Buxton expended 370 rounds to 'flame' a Bv 138, while ten days later Sub-Lts Machin and Davies dispatched a second. Then, working the next JW/RA convoy, No 835, off *Nairana*, splashed another Blohm und Voss on 12 December. Despite poor visibility and rapidly-fading light, Sub-Lt Gordon made the kill with merely 60 rounds per gun.

JW- and RA-64 in February 1945 provided repeated opportunities, but frustrating results, for Nos 813 and 835 Sqns. Still embarked in *Campania* and *Nairana*, respectively, they were augmented by a solitary Fulmar nightfighter in *Campania*. The Wildcats were vectored onto half-a-dozen bogeys, only two of which were confirmed destroyed. No 813 splashed a Ju 88 on 6 February, but lost a fighter and its pilot in the process, cause unknown. Three more Junkers were intercepted on the 10th, during which the Grummans fired nearly 4000 rounds. However, the Germans' speed and good use of clouds limited claims to a probable, one possible and a damaged. No 835's sharpshooting D G Gordon, who had proven so efficient on 12 December, was back in form on 20 February. He and Sub-Lt P H Blanco required only 260 rounds of .50 cal to destroy a snooping Ju 88. Meanwhile, another section on the opposite side of the convoy probably splashed another.

One of the Wildcat's last battles in Royal Navy service was perhaps the most intriguing of all. On 26 March 1945 *Searcher*'s No 882 Sqn escorted an Avenger strike along the Norwegian coast in company with other carrier aircraft. Eight Bf 109Gs attacked beneath an overcast, gaining the initial advantage by damaging one Wildcat Mk VI. The

Few Wildcats wore D-Day invasion strips as most aircraft were involved elsewhere on Russian convoy patrols, Norwegian coastal strikes or Mediterranean and Far East deployments. However, one unit that was very much in the thick of things over Normandy was No 846 Sqn, embarked on HMS *Tracker*. The unit primarily flew in support of Avengers, also from No 846 Sqn, in anti-shipping strikes up and down the Channel. This machine, an Eastern-built Mk V, bears the legend, 'That Old Thing', in yellow above the wing, and is seen cruising along the English south coast in late June 1944 (*via Aeroplane*)

One of the FAA's first Wildcat Mk VIs is put through its paces in Britain, prior to being issued to a frontline squadron in the autumn of 1944. Equivalent to the US Navy's FM-2, Wildcat VIs served primarily in the Far East, although the first squadron to re-equip with the type was No 881, very much a Home Fleet unit from the Martlet's earliest days (*via Phil Jarrett*)

low-level combat was resolved in favour of the Grumman's manoeuvrability, however, with four Messerschmitts being claimed destroyed and one damaged.

Only four days before the war in Europe ended, FAA Wildcats flew their last mission against Germany. Three CVEs – *Queen*, *Searcher* and *Tracker* – launched 44 sorties against Kilbotn, in Norway, which sank two ships and a U-boat. Wildcat flak suppression limited losses to one fighter and an Avenger on 4 May.

On VJ-Day in September 1945 the FAA boasted 1179 carrier aircraft – five times the number of six years before. Of those, only No 882 Sqn at Cochin was still flying Wildcats – 24 Mk VIs intended for *Searcher*.

The Fleet Air Arm produced some 16 aces, including those seconded to the RAF. However, very few scored five or more victories in any one FAA aircraft type. Lt C C Tomkinson's 2.5 (all Vichy French aircraft shot down over northern Madagascar in May 1942 whilst the pilot was attached to No 881 Sqn) remained the highest score for the Martlet/Wildcat, while No 882 Sqn was the most successful unit with seven kills. For comparison, here are the top scores in other FAA fighters:

Fulmar	Lt Cdr S G Orr	No 806 Sqn	8.50
Sea Hurricane	Lt Cdr R A Brabner,	No 801 Sqn	5
Sea Gladiator	Cdr C L Keighly-Peach,	HMS *Eagle* Flight	3.50
Corsair	Lt D J Sheppard,	No 1836 Sqn	5
Skua	Lt Cdr W P Lucy,	No 803 Sqn	3.33
Hellcat	Sub-Lt E T Wilson,	No 1844 Sqn	4.83
Seafire	Sub-Lt R Reynolds,	No 894 Sqn	3.50

Despite this apparent disparity in individual scores, the Martlet/Wildcat showed very favourably in total victories credited. The 54 attributed to the type was exceeded in the Royal Navy only by the Fulmar. The difference is explained by the exceptional variety of service provided by 1082 Martlets/Wildcats flying with more than 30 squadrons from 1940 to 1945. No other FAA fighter enjoyed so long a wartime career, nor did any other achieve victories over all four major Axis air forces: Germany, Italy, Vichy France and Japan.

PILOT PROFILE -
CAPTAIN ERIC 'WINKLE' BROWN,
CBE, DSC, AFC, RN

As detailed above, the Fleet Air Arm produced very few aces during World War 2, principally because the 'Senior Service' employed its aerial assets on a mix of convoy protection and ground attack tasks. When enemy aircraft were encountered, dedicated RAF (in Europe) or US Navy (Indian and Pacific Oceans) fighter units would usually neutralise any attacks. Therefore, if the strict rules of 'acedom' – five kills – are to be applied, then the pilot featured in this monograph should not be included, as he finished the war with only two confirmed kills and a probable to his credit. This nevertheless ranked him closely behind the most successful Martlet pilot of the war, Lt C C Tomkinson.

However, statistics often hide as much of the true picture as they reveal, and the combat experience of Capt Eric 'Winkle' Brown is a perfect example of this. He was flying Martlet Is and IIs on convoy patrols three months *prior* to the Japanese raid on Pearl Harbor, claiming kills weeks before the US Marine Corps opened their account over Wake Island.

Brown's pre-war flying on Gloster Gauntlet biplane fighters with the Edinburgh University Air Squadron taught him the basics of aerial combat in the relaxed surroundings of a nation at peace, albeit steadily preparing for war. Many of his contemporaries within the FAA were lost early in the first three years of the conflict due to a general lack of experience, principally because time did not then allow pilots to spend many months sharpening their skills prior to entering frontline service.

Upon the outbreak of war, Brown voluntarily switched services to the Navy, and after initially flying Sea Gladiators, he was posted to No 802 Sqn at Donibristle, in Fife, where he flew the less than inspiring Blackburn fighters, the Skua and the Roc. Fortunately, he was never forced to go into combat in either type, and in early 1941 his squadron became the first unit within the FAA to receive Martlets, these machines being ex-French *Aéronavale* G-36As that had been diverted to Britain following the fall of France three months earlier. Thus began his brief association with the Grumman fighter.

The following interview was conducted in August 1994 specially for this volume, and Capt Brown's memories of his Martlet flying provide a uniquely British angle to the Wildcat/Martlet story.

'The first thing that struck us about these Martlet Is, or G-36s, to give them their correct designation, was that the instrumentation within the cockpit was still in metric units! Nevertheless, we were still very impressed for this aircraft, from our point of view, was really the bridge between the biplane and the monoplane.

'Up to that point we had had some real rubbish in the Fleet Air Arm, and you really couldn't call our previous aircraft, the Roc, a fighter at all. We also had plenty of biplanes like the Sea Gladiator and the Swordfish, but both types were by now very outdated. Therefore, we were very happy to see this "creature" arrive on the scene.

'We were being prepared to go aboard the Navy's first escort carrier, HMS *Empire Audacity*, although we didn't know this at the time. This new weapon of war was the child of Churchill's genius – he had the idea that if we could get a suitable merchant ship and literally slice the top off it and put a flight deck on it, we could operate suitable aircraft in the convoy protection role.

'We couldn't spare the bigger carriers for this task as they were needed elsewhere. This first escort carrier was, in fact, an ex-German banana boat (SS *Hannover*) which had been captured in the West Indies. It was brought back to the UK and had had a flight deck of 423 ft in length built over its hull. There was no hangar, so all six (later eight) Martlets had to be ranged on the deck. They took up further usable take-off space for launching aircraft – so much so that the first pilot to launch on a mission had only about 300 ft of deck to take-off from.

'Prior to embarkation we spent

A youthful Sub-Lt Eric 'Winkle' Brown clutches onto his gloves and maps as he makes his way to the stern of *Audacity*, where his Martlet II is being prepared for its next patrol over Gibraltar-bound convoy OG-74. This snapshot was taken by a fellow No 802 Sqn pilot in early October 1941 – the squadron had already made their presence felt by this stage in the cruise, having destroyed a Fw 200 a fortnight before. Brown and his fellow pilots never flew in their Irvin jackets, as worn here, due to the fact that they quickly became water-logged in the event of a ditching, and could easily drag the wearer down to a watery grave. However, they proved adept at staving off the inclement weather up on deck prior to launching on patrol *(via Capt E Brown)*

Few photographs of the converted German merchantman HMS *Empress Audacity* were taken prior to her brief career commencing in September 1941. This side-on shot clearly shows her 'islandless' flightdeck and tactical 'dazzle' paint scheme *(via Capt E Brown)*

much of the spring and summer of 1941 flying intensive work-ups with the Martlet Mk Is, and later Mk IIs, in the Fife area. The RAF were also quite interested in the fighter at the time, from both a recognition point of view and also as a dissimilar dogfighting opponent for their Hurricanes (pincipally those from RAF Digby) and Spitfires. It handled itself well against both types, being very comparable overall to the Hawker fighter. If anything, it was perhaps more rugged than the Hurricane, but it didn't share the latter's impressive rate of roll. However, the Martlet had a startling initial rate of climb, although the higher it got the more the Hurricane caught it up. The Martlet was built for medium to low level work, and to emphasise this point none had oxygen fitted to them.

'With this positive dogfighting experience under our belts we felt confident that we could more than hold our own against the Luftwaffe fighters of the day, and were very disappointed that we never got a crack at them. However, in light of the US Navy's experience with the Zero, which proved near impossible to counter in a turning fight, and our post-war evaluation of the Fw 190, it was perhaps just as well that we never encountered these fighters in our Martlet IIs. To help us deal with our known targets – Kondors – we also had a spell of fighter liaison with a Halifax bomber squadron prior to our deployment. The primary aim of this exercise was essentially to teach you how much the slipstream of these big aircraft could toss you around if you attempted a stern attack.

'We eventually got aboard in September 1941, the squadron embarking eight pilots and six aircraft. Once at sea on this historic trip, we found ourselves on the North Atlantic to Gibraltar run, which passed through some of the roughest water in the world. This really wasn't ideal, operationally speaking, for a small ship like ours as you got a lot of heavy flight deck movement.

'To illustrate how bad this was, on one occasion we measured that the ship's stern was rising and falling through a total arc of 65 feet. It also rolled as well as pitched, and we lost an aircraft off the deck on operations during our second patrol, performed in early November 1941, when the ship rolled over eight degrees from neutral – this, of course, was occurring both to port and starboard.

'The stern was heaving heavily on this particular occasion, and after one attempted landing by the unfortunate pilot, he was struck by the deck on the "up swing" as he came over the stern on his second recovery. It hit the aircraft square on, and literally tossed it overboard. Fortunately, the Martlet's inherent floatation characteristics then came into play, the in-built buoyancy bags fitted in the wings inflating as soon as their activating hydrostatic valves came in contact with the water.

'Our task was to carry out constant patrols round the convoy looking out for surfaced U-boats, which performed much of their attack work on the surface until close to the convoy itself. The Focke-Wulf Fw

This truly remarkable photograph, borrowed from Capt Brown's own private scrapbook, shows him leading his section in a rather unorthodox fashion whilst undertaking an interception over the Atlantic in September 1941. The shot itself was taken by the pilot of a Pan American Boeing 314, nicknamed 'Dixie Clipper', which was flying a routine passenger run between the Azores and Lisbon, in Portugal. At the time the US was still neutral, and the skipper of the flying boat took serious umbrage to being intercepted at close quarters by the trio of No 802 Sqn fighters. He duly sent his photographic handiwork to the American Embassy in Lisbon, who in turn forwarded it to the London consulate. From there, it finally reached the Admiralty, who instructed a young Sub-Lt Brown's commanding officer to reprimand him. 'Winkle' duly lost three months seniority in rank for, as his boss wryly told him, 'a lapse of concentration in the duty that you were supposed to be fulfilling'. Eric's section mates on this patrol were, to starboard, Sub-Lt Graham 'Fletch' Fletcher and, to port, Sub-Lt Bertie Williams *(via Capt E Brown)*

200 Kondors were very active relaying to the U-boats the positions of convoys, as well as bombing any straggling elements of the flotilla itself.

'We had quite a busy time with the Kondors during this period, and, despite our best efforts, they had their successes against us, not only from the viewpoint of good reconnaissance reporting. On our second convoy patrol (OG-76), a Fw 200 succeeded in shooting down our CO, Lt Cdr John Wintour, who, upon setting the Kondor alight, thought he had inflicted the *coup de grace* on the Focke-Wulf and drew up alongside the aircraft to survey the situation, whereupon the dorsal gunner promptly shot him down.

'I inadvertently chanced upon the best angle of attack against a Kondor during my first encounter with the type on 8 November 1941, although I have to confess to having thought about this approach prior to this engagement. Indeed, we had even discussed the head-on attack in the crew room aboard ship, but dismissed it because we never thought that we would have a sufficient speed advantage to overhaul the Fw 200, unless of course we were vectored in from head on from the start. I had a belief that the forward dorsal turret couldn't depress its guns below a certain angle, and, similarly, the ventral gondola couldn't elevate its guns to cover the "blind spot" either. This blank area ahead could then be exploited providing you came in very flat.

'I only resorted to this form of attack after my frustrated efforts at textbook beam and quarter attacks had failed to make any impression, other than to set the starboard inner engine alight, and I lost him in cloud. This pilot, as with most other Kondor crews that we encountered, also resorted to the favoured tactic of turning into me every time I ran in to attack – when I made the head-on pass he just flew straight on at me, keeping the Kondor straight and level so as to give the gunners a stable platform from which to aim from.

'After several minutes we eventually broke back in to clear skies head-on to each other! I closed on him with the flattest possible trajectory, being careful not to stray into his forward firing zones. We had six .50 cal machine guns in our Martlet Mk IIs, which sprayed out a fair amount of lead, and I could actually see the windscreen of the Kondor disintegrating in front of me as I closed on the bomber. These guns were a revelation to us as they were a far heavier calibre than we had ever previously used.

'Our convoy patrols were usually performed in pairs at 1000 ft at a speed of around 150 kts, and we only "opened up" when we saw the chance of potential action. One had a lot of confidence in the Martlet, which was just as well really as we were flying a single-engined aircraft over water 800 miles from any land bases. To make matters worse, if you did ditch some distance from the carrier, it was unlikely that a vessel could be spared from the convoy to come and pick you up.

'To this end, we tended to do the patrol with the convoy just in sight, one of us going clockwise and the other anti-clockwise. We weren't allowed to talk on the radio at all, unless of course it was an emergency – for example, if we spotted a U-boat running into attack the convoy. It was, therefore, a very peculiar existence just flying around in large circles in complete silence. We were flying the Mk II Martlet by this stage which was powered by the very smooth Twin Wasp radial engine, which gave off a confidence-boosting "purr" when running properly.

'*Audacity* only completed three-and-a-half legs of convoy protection duty before we were "hacked" on the return trip with HG-76 on the night of 20/21 December 1941 by U-751. During this entire period I intercepted three Kondors, destroying two and losing the third in cloud. The weather was always dreadful during our time aboard the carrier, with thick cloud cover usually aiding the Luftwaffe crews on almost all interceptions.

'From a No 802 Sqn perspective, we had three sections (two aircraft) on the first convoy patrol we performed, and they all experienced at least one contact, and four sections on the second, which again all crossed swords with the Luftwaffe. On the odd occasion we were also shot at by "friendlies", usually Coastal Command Sunderlands and Liberator Is. We were also scrambled to intercept civilian Boeing Clipper flying boats flying the Lisbon-Azores route, these slow contacts usually being picked up first as blips on *Audacity*'s radar, and unidentifiable as to type.

'Aside from our standing patrol, which would be sent off to investigate any contacts approaching the convoy, we also maintained two Martlets on the deck at immediate readiness, with pilots strapped in. A further pair were then on standby. The squadron had four pairs of crews for its six aircraft, with the final pairing being classed as available at five minutes' notice. This allowed them to get their heads down after having performed a patrol, or a long spell at alert on the pitching deck.

The alert aircraft had their engines kept warm by brief engine runs every half-hour, and as soon as word came through to launch it was simply a matter of actuating the inertia starter switch and flying off the carrier once it had been turned into wind. Occasionally we would even launch when the ship was still steering into wind. We used flap on launch, and as the Martlet had no intermediate flap setting – it was either up or down – we modified the moveable surfaces by inserting small wooden blocks (like wedge door stops) when the flaps were fully open whilst the aircraft was idle on the deck. It was then closed up to the blocks, giving us 20 degrees of flap, which helped our climb out from take-off immensely. As you climbed out you opened the flaps even further and the blocks simply fell away!

'Workload was very heavy in the Martlet straight after take-off as the undercarriage had to be hand-cranked shut. This took 29 turns, and you had to be careful not to snag you R/T helmet lead around the handle. One pilot had crashed his aircraft only weeks after the first Martlet Is had arrived in Scotland when he got himself tangled up and wound his head down into the cockpit.

'The maintenance section aboard ship worked miracles with our Martlets as all rectification work had to take place out in the open on the flight deck, usually at night. These chaps struggled just to keep their footing on the invariably wet and heaving deck, and because they weren't allowed to show lights at night so as to avoid detection by U-boats, they operated with hand torches which had had the bulbs covered with blue

The calm before the storm – a group of recently-embarked No 802 Sqn sub-lieutenants and a pair of armourers pose for the camera just prior to *Audacity* joining up with OG-74. Sitting in the cockpit is Norris 'Pat' Patterson who, along with 'Fletch' Fletcher (no cap in photo), shared the first unit kill of the cruise on 21 September 1941 when they destroyed a Fw 200 of KG 40. Fletcher was killed by a flak battery aboard *U-131* on *Audacity*'s second patrol, whilst the remaining trio ('Sheepy' Lamb, left, and 'Bertie' Williams, right) also died in later combat *(via Capt E Brown)*

Firmly harnessed into his Martlet II, Sub-Lt Brown sits on the rolling deck of *Audacity*, awaiting the call to scramble. Endless hours could be spent sitting in the damp cockpit environment of a lashed down Martlet whilst the standing patrol droned tirelessly about overhead *(via Capt E Brown)*

paper. Even then, they were not allowed to put these on until they were in a compartment or in the cockpit. Despite these harsh conditions, they never complained due to their total dedication to the job, and they were No 802 Sqn's real heroes.

Fortunately, we didn't bend our Martlets too often despite the weather, which kept heavy maintenance for the engineering section down to a minimum. This was due primarily to the aircraft's marvellous landing characteristics, aided by the self-centring arrester wires fitted to the carrier. The undercarriage on the aircraft was also very "mushy", which allowed it to absorb high vertical velocities without producing any rebound reactions. We also enjoyed an excellent forward view of the carrier on approach to landing, and the Martlet's innocuous stall characteristics meant that you could fly it right down to the lower speed limits during a recovery without too many worries. This machine really could not have been bettered for the job at hand in late 1941.

'In all the time I operated the Martlet the only real feedback we got from the US regarding our aircraft concerned Grumman's attempts at Bethpage to solve the take-off swing experienced when operating from land bases. No in-service evaluations or reports from US Navy squadrons ever reached us to my knowledge. The manufacturer let it be known to us they were planning on replacing the solid tail wheel with a longer oleo fitted with a pneumatic type. Conversely, we learnt through the US Embassy in London that their Navy were very interested to hear how the .50 cal machine gun behaved in combat. They wanted to know if we were suffering high stoppage rates, and if so, were we able to clear the guns with the cocking handles. We never saw any engineers or representatives from Grumman up in Scotland!

'We reported back to the Americans that we were impressed with the spread of fire with the guns, and the accuracy we achieved through a combination of the aircraft's remarkable stability – if anything, the Martlet was *too* stable to be a fighter – and its superb gunsight, made our gunnery scores very respectable. We suffered stoppages, but nothing too severe.

'The Martlet really was ideally suited to carrier aviation, and I've yet to meet an ex-F4F/FM-2 pilot who has anything bad to say about the aircraft. One thing often forgotten when discussing aircraft of this type, is the peace of mind derived by the pilot from flying a machine with good deck landing characteristics. In operations you have the stress of the combat, and with land operations once that climax is over all you then have to do is get yourself back to the airfield. In naval aviation, a), you've got to first find your carrier, and directions were rarely given, with most navigation being done by simple dead-reckoning in total radio silence; and b), once you did find it, getting back aboard a vessel that, more often than not, was pitching and rolling about quite heavily. So you really had three distinct periods of extremely high stress to deal with per flight.'

One of the lesser known wartime actions undertaken by the FAA saw two squadrons of Wildcats support a massed Allied force invading the South of France in August 1944 as part of Operation *Anvil-Dragoon*. Although no aerial opposition was encountered, these Wildcat Mk VIs of No 881 Sqn nevertheless made their presence felt by undertaking dozens of ground attack missions equipped with 250 lb bombs. This busy photograph shows squadron machines being readied for the next wave of sorties from HMS *Pursuer*, bombs being fitted to the Wildcats' inner wing pylons. Immediately behind the pilot's head in the middle of this shot is a rare example of FAA wartime nose art, here taking the form of a female rabbit *(via Aeroplane)*

TRAINING

While there has always been an aura of glamour surrounding military flying, the path to pilot's wings has never been easy. Perhaps the sentiment was best expressed in a training manual which stated, 'Naval aviation is not a sport. It is a scientific profession'. The needs of that profession were expanding dramatically in 1941, striving to provide tens of thousands of pilots, aircrew, maintenance and support personnel for the growing threat of war. While concessions to increased need were implemented, a high standard was still maintained and met – one student pilot in three failed to complete flight training.

The syllabus was altered considerably during the war years, but those pilots in fleet squadrons at the time of Pearl Harbor had already survived a gruelling year-long course at NAS Pensacola, Florida. There the cadets advanced through five squadrons, beginning on Naval Aircraft Factory N3N floatplanes and progressing to either the wheeled versions of the N3N or the Boeing-Stearman N2S. Eventually the aviation cadets (AvCads) graduated to North American SNJs, then seaplanes such as Consolidated PBYs, and finally to obsolescent fighters like the Boeing F4B. Upon graduation and commissioning as ensigns or Marine second lieutenants, the new aviators had logged some 300 or more flight hours.

Before establishment of the Carrier Qualification Training Unit (CQTU) at NAS Glenview, Illinois, in 1942, those fliers assigned to fighters learned their trade in their fleet squadrons. Pre-war fighter pilots also conducted individual battle practice (IBP), learning air combat from more experienced fliers.

Occasionally it was necessary to take down an overconfident youngster one or two rungs. Some of the 'old hands' resorted to potentially humiliating tactics – dogfighting while eating an apple, or even 'reading' a newspaper! Then, as now, combat proficiency was an evolutionary experience. So too was learning the fine points of aerial gunnery. The aim of every fledgling fighter pilot was to qualify as an 'expert', thus winning the right to paint the gunnery 'E' on his assigned aeroplane.

Meanwhile, a 'finishing school' had been established at NAS North Island, San Diego. Beginning in the summer of 1941, the Aircraft Carrier

An extremely loose formation of nondescript F4F-4s cruise at medium altitude during a training sortie over California on 26 March 1943. The general appearance of these fighters reflects the far less strenuous existence enjoyed by the Aircraft Carrier Training Group units, whose groundcrews could afford to spend a little more time maintaining their fighters within the luxury of permanent hangars at stations like NAS San Diego and the USMC's Camp Kearney. Virtually all Wildcats used by the training groups were 'war-weary' aircraft shipped back from the Pacific Theatre, and on at least one occasion an F4F-4 that had allegedly been flown by Joe Foss at Guadalcanal was issued to a Mojave, California, based unit. New pilots going through training at the base recall that the battered Wildcat sported 20 or more victory flags. However, it had most likely been successful in the hands of several pilots *(via Phil Jarrett)*

Training Group (ACTG) taught the basics of carrier flying with a cadre of experienced instructors. Despite its name, ACTG was concerned with more than just flying off and landing aboard carriers. For fighter pilots, tactical instruction was also a part of the curriculum, concentrating on aerial gunnery.

After Pearl Harbor all big-deck carriers were committed to combat, and few escort carriers were available for training. And since the onset of winter precluded instruction on the Great Lakes, Carrier Qualification Training Unit moved to San Diego until the spring. Eventually, two modified cruise boats were commissioned for carrier training on Lake Michigan: USS *Wolverine* (IX-64) and *Sable* (IX-81) in August 1942 and April 1943, respectively. Fledgling carrier pilots qualified with eight landings, either in SNJ trainers or fleet aircraft such as F4Fs, SBDs or TBFs.

Though autonomous from 1939, the Fleet Air Arm still relied heavily upon the RAF for training through much of the war. The Commonwealth Air Training Plan produced thousands of aircrew, not only in Great Britain, but in Canada, Australia, India and South Africa. Other Royal Navy pilots won their wings at NAS Pensacola. Those who passed through the RAF schools then went to FAA training units for specialised instruction in naval procedures and, of course, carrier operations.

Leadership has always been the crucial element in military affairs, and whatever failings F4F squadrons faced in their equipment was amply compensated for by their commanding officers. The nearly 20 Navy and Marine squadrons which flew Wildcats in Pacific combat during 1942 possessed an almost uniformly high standard of leadership – mostly Annapolis-trained professional officers with considerable aviation experience.

Many of these men are well known to history: John S Thach (VF-3), James H Flatley, Jr (VF-10), John L Smith (VMF-223), Robert E Galer (VMF-224) and Harold W Bauer (VMF-212) being the most familiar. However, others such as Paul H Ramsey (VF-2), Leroy C Simpler (VF-5), Louis H Bauer (VF-6), Charles R Fenton (VF-42) and Leonard K Davis (VMF-121) produced competent and motivated squadrons. Their methods varied widely, from the thorough professionalism of a Flatley to the flint-edged demeanor of a Smith; from the flamboyance of a Ramsey to the quiet competence of a Galer. Most of the highly-successful fighter skippers were born teachers, 'Jimmy' Thach, 'Jim' Flatley and 'Indian Joe' Bauer being prime examples.

But regardless of their personalities or methods, all of these men shared one common trait – they subscribed to the classic military technique of leading from the front. Few of them were the best pilots in their units, but nearly all made efficient use of the human resources available to them. Additionally, the finest leaders shared one other characteristic – they took care of their subordinates, both in the air and on the ground. Fifty years later, intelligent commanders still follow their example.

By late 1943, the few remaining F4F-4s in Navy service had been relegated to second-line training squadrons in the US. Their they were used and abused by the next generation of Wildcat pilots who would fly the far more potent FM-2 into combat. These aircraft all wear suitably large training codes, as well as the briefly used (from July to October 1943, to be precise) red 'star and bar' surrounds. This fine shot was officially released to the press by the US Navy on 26 October 1943 *(via Aeroplane)*

VICTORY CREDITS AND WILDCAT EVALUATION

When the Pacific War began, the US naval service had no standard method of evaluating or crediting aerial victories. However, the increasing tempo of air combat in early 1942 required that such methods be adopted, and individual air groups produced their own means of reporting combat action. The result generally was a mimeographed sheet of paper with standard questions, and room for amplifying drawings.

Aerial victory credits were generally assessed at unit level, unlike the USAAF tier of evaluation boards. The Navy method was largely dictated by the physical environment in which F4F units operated – from aircraft carriers or remote airfields. Thus, most victory claims were taken at face value, and so noted in a pilot's logbook. However, by the Battle of Midway, apparently some Navy fighting squadrons invoked an internal check upon initial claims. In that battle the three F4F squadrons claimed 45 kills – they actually got 29, or about two-thirds of what they claimed.

That ratio fits the historical average. As a general rule, western air forces tend to overclaim by *at least* a factor of one-third. Thus, for every three kills credited, approximately two enemy aircraft were generally shot down. Examination of individual squadrons' records shows that claims become more accurate with experience. Among F4F squadrons, the trend was most evident with the Marines on Guadalcanal. Their initial claims were usually well off the mark, but with a diminishing error factor as pilots observed genuine kills as a means of comparison. However, conditions on Guadalcanal conspired against accurate records – a scarcity of paper, coupled with increasing fatigue among all hands. Additionally, many unit histories or reports were only compiled after leaving the island.

One aspect of 1942 victory credits remains largely unexplained: the frequent credit of an ' assist'. Apparently the term had different meanings in different units. Sometimes, an assist was considered as a fractional credit wherein two or more pilots contributed to downing a hostile. Other times, 'assist' merely indicated that a fighter pilot contributed in some way to a successful combat. The term seems to have died out in late 1942, replaced by fractional credits.

As inaccurate as American victory claims could be at times, they were almost never as wildly inflated as their opponents'. The Japanese Navy consistently overclaimed by orders of magnitude, to the point that historians have concluded that an institutional optimism pervaded IJN fighter units! If a Zero pilot fired at an Allied aircraft, the target was apparently considered at least probably destroyed.

Perhaps the best-known instance of this involved the 107-aircraft attack on Midway on the morning of 4 June. Zeros engaged 25 F2As and F4Fs, destroying 15 in a quarter of an hour. However, upon returning to their carriers the Zero pilots claimed 40 'destroyed' and numerous 'probables' – all F4Fs. In turn, the Marines were credited with 11 shootdowns against the enemy's 10 actual losses. The fact that AA fire also destroyed several Japanese aircraft makes respective credits difficult to allocate.

In the end, the numerical claims of air combat – 'the score' – mattered less than the aftermath. If enemy losses in destroyed and damaged aircraft prevented him from launching another strike, that was what counted most. During 1942, outright aerial supremacy seldom existed for either side after Coral Sea. But the results attained by Navy and Marine F4F squadrons increasingly swung air superiority in favour of the Americans. The long-range results proved irrevocable for the Empire of Japan.

By VJ-Day, the total Wildcat score stood at 1514.5 aerial victories credited to US units. They broke down by service and type as follows:

US Marine F4Fs	(11 squadrons)	562 victories
US Navy F4Fs	(28 squadrons)	520.5 victories
US Navy FMs	(38 squadrons)	432 victories

Of 76 Wildcat units credited with victories, the top 15 were:

VMF-121	Solomons	160
VMF-223	Solomons	133.5 (22.5 TAD)
VF-5	*Saratoga* and Solomons	79
VGF-11/VF-21	Solomons	69
VC-27	*Savo Island*	61.5
VMF-224	Solomons	61.5 (6.5 TAD)
VMF-112	Solomons	61
VMF-212	Solomons	57
VF-11	Solomons	55
VF-3	*Lexington, Yorktown*	50.5 (some as VF-42)
VGF/VF-26	*Sangamon*, Solomons and *Santee*	46
VF-72	*Hornet* and Solomons	44
VF-10	*Enterprise* and Solomons	43
VMO-251	Solomons	33
VMF-221	Solomons	30

Unique among all Wildcat squadrons was VF-26, which began as VGF-26 aboard *Sangamon* and claimed four Vichy aircraft during Operation *Torch*. Redesignated VF-26 and sent to the Pacific in 1943, the squadron logged a further 11 victories while land-based in the Solomons. Finally, though functioning as a VC unit, VF-26 flew FM-2s aboard *Santee* in 1944. In the latter capacity the squadron ranked second among all CVE units with 31 kills, primarily in the Philippines campaign. No other squadron drew Axis blood while flying Wildcats for three consecutive years.

F4F/FM-2 Evaluated

After the Battle of Midway, Lt Cdr John Thach said that, 'Only fighters can keep our aircraft carriers afloat'. The increasing importance of fighters in the composition of carrier air groups bore out Thach's assessment, as F4F numbers steadily increased. At the time of Pearl Harbor, each carrier fighter unit possessed 18 aircraft. By Midway the number was 27 – a 50 per cent increase in six months. At the start of the Guadalcanal campaign the carriers nominally had 36 F4Fs apiece. The trend would only continue as the war progressed closer to Japan. By 1945 the new-generation *Essex*-class ships embarked a staggering 73 Hellcats or Corsairs, including nightfighter and photo-reconnaissance detachments.

Whatever its performance deficiencies, the F4F possessed one supreme advantage – availability. During the crucial summer of 1942, the F6F was a full year from combat deployment and the F4U was more than six months away from arriving at Guadalcanal. In that respect the Wildcat was the Navy counterpart to the USAAF's Curtiss P-40. However, attrition nearly matched production. From July through November 1942, Pacific Fleet carrier fighter squadrons received 197 Wildcats, including a few recce-F4F-7s. Losses to all causes were 115, or 58 per cent – small wonder then that back on Long Island, Grumman was working no less than three shifts.

In contrast to the Hellcat and Corsair, the Wildcat lacked two endearing characteristics as seen from the command level – range and payload. The former was particularly important in the war's largest arena, as many Navy and Marine Corps strike missions were flown beyond the F4F's radius of action. The fact that most such missions succeeded was a testimony to the skill and dedication of unescorted SBD and TBF crews, who often faced enemy fighters alone.

Wildcats were seldom called upon to perform genuine strike missions, though bombs and rockets were occasionally used. In both large carriers and CVEs, other aircraft (most notably TBF/TBM Avengers) were dedicated to the attack role. Therefore, the F4F's minimal strike potential was seldom a serious drawback, though certainly the type lacked the versatility of later fighters.

Unquestionably, the F4F – and to a lesser extent the FM – was best employed in the air-defense role. Flying both from carriers and from Guadalcanal, Wildcats were most effectively used to deter or minimise the effects of Japanese attack aircraft – horizontal and dive bombers, as well as torpedo planes. Certainly the aces' best missions were flown against enemy bombers – especially Aichi D3A 'Vals'. Of the eight F4F aces in a day, O'Hare, Vejtasa, Wrenn and Swett scored against bombers, as did FM pilots Hippe and Funk.

Despite the service's institutional reluctance to popularise individual fighter pilots, some aviators became well known. The Navy produced 25 F4F/FM aces and the Marines 34, eight of whom were killed during the war. Butch O'Hare remained the only carrier-based F4F pilot awarded the Medal of Honor, but Guadalcanal-based Marines were showered with decorations. Smith,

The FM-2 was the ultimate Wildcat to see service from the wooden decks of the US Navy's burgeoning carrier escort force. As part of its accelerated clearance trials prior to the type being issued to frontline units, this early production airframe was put through its paces by the NAS Patuxent River test establishment – its ownership is detailed in the small stencilled writing beneath the cockpit. The star and bar is outlined in red, dating this shot as having been taken in July 1943, and the hastily scrawled number eight on the nose and tail was added specifically for 'spotting', or parking, purposes whilst the FM-2 was at sea *(via Phil Jarrett)*

Galer, Bauer and Foss all received the Medal of Honor for 1942 combat, while DeBlanc and Swett were recognised for their early 1943 records. Combined with the posthumous postwar award to Major Elrod of Wake Island, eight F4F pilots received America's highest military decoration – more than were presented to pilots of any other single-engine aircraft flown by US armed forces in the war.

The British Admiralty was less concerned with the Grumman's range and strike limitations than the US Navy Bureau of Aeronautics. As noted previously, the Wildcat's greatest selling point to the Royal Navy was its respectable performance and robust construction. With no other single-seat fighter designed as a carrier aircraft from the ground up, the FAA was more than pleased with the Martlet. Flight-deck crews also appreciated the American 'tail-down' means of catapult launch at a time when most British carrier aircraft required a cradle for the 'tail-up' method of shooting machines off the 'booster'.

WEAPONS

It has been said that the guns are the 'soul' of a fighter. In the Wildcat that meant the superb M2 Browning .50 cal, arguably the finest aircraft weapon of the war.

The F4F-3/3A series was armed with four .50 cals, each with 450 rounds per gun, thus making a total of 1800 shells. However, with the advent of the folding-wing F4F-4 in late 1941, the US standard of six M2s was employed. Oddly, the 'improved' armament was instigated by the Royal Navy, which by then had ordered 220 Martlet Mk IVs. Between the wing-fold mechanism and the extra guns, ammunition capacity was reduced to 240 rounds per gun, or 1440 total. To fighter pilots, the difference was substantial: the 'dash four' was heavier and slower than the F4F-3, with only some 18 seconds firing time – barely half the older Wildcat's.

The deficit was eventually redressed in the FM-2, which reverted to the four-gun package which had proven satisfactory in the early 1942 battles. Additionally, the FM's frequent close air support role was enhanced by this additional ammunition, which allowed more time on station before 'firing out'.

Essentially, US Navy fighter squadrons used two methods in aligning their guns. Probably most common was convergence of all six weapons around a point 1000 ft ahead of the fighter. The size of the circle varied from squadron to squadron, but three mils was certainly as small as any one cared to use. In that case, three mils subtended three ft at 1000 ft range, for a pattern one yard in diameter.

However, only an expert aerial gunner could make good use of a three-mil harmonisation. Most pilots were not so proficient, and consequently, a wider dispersion was developed by boresighting each set of guns at different ranges: usually 250, 300 and 350 yards for outboard, middle and inboard guns, respectively. This 'pattern boresight' was attributed to Lt Cdr Gordon Cady, who flew F4Fs with VF-11 at Guadalcanal during 1943. Though inherently less lethal than the tighter cone of fire, its greater dispersion of lead made some hits more likely, which could often have a telling effect in any case due to the fact that Japanese aircraft lacked both airframe armour and self-sealing tanks.

The US Navy was probably the only air arm in the world which regularly practiced full-deflection aerial gunnery. In order to shoot effectively at high target-crossing angles, reflector sights were developed, replacing the tubular variety left over from the biplane era. In F4Fs the most common sights were the N-2 and Mk VIII types, with the latter eventually becoming standard. It featured a centre dot, or 'pipper', subtending one mil, with 50- and 100-mil radii to help calculate deflection. The rule of thumb was called the 'two-thirds rule', in which the correct lead at boresight range (1000 ft) was two-thirds the target speed in knots. Thus, a 300-knot enemy aircraft engaged from broad on the beam required a 200-mil hold-off.

Fleet Air Arm practice largely paralleled American usage – not surprising, considering that identical weapons were employed. The standard Admiralty harmonisation was 250 yards, though evidently without the overlapping pattern boresight favoured by the US Navy. Similarly, Martlets widely employed the standard US Mk VIII optical sight, with centre pipper surrounded by 50- and 100-mil rings.

Where variety existed in FAA use, it seems to have been in the different squadrons' choice of ammunition sequencing. When No 802 Sqn embarked in *Audacity* in 1941 their Mk IIs were loaded with one armour-piercing (AP) round for every four ball. During 1943, No 800 Sqn's Martlet Mk IVs loaded incendiary rounds in the inboard and outboard guns, with AP in the middle weapon. However, during the same period No 881 Sqn's Mk IIs employed five rounds ball to two AP. With the return of the four-gun armament in Mk Vs and VIs, standard loading was incendiary inboard and outboard AP. Some squadrons accomplished the same purpose by by utilising a mix of AP and incendiary rounds in the same belts.

Special-mission considerations occasionally show up in action reports. For instance, in early 1944 No 882's Mk Vs loaded one gun with tracer and AP to aid in sighting while strafing. At the time of the squadron's combat with Bf 109s in March 1945 the belting was 20 incendiary, 20 AP, 20 tracer and 20 ball. Otherwise, FAA fighters apparently did not widely use tracers.

Aside from air-to-air gunnery and strafing, Wildcats seldom employed weapons other than guns. However, both F4Fs and FMs demonstrated an ability to put other ordnance on target – sometimes under dire circumstances. Ironically, the F4F's most successful attack missions were flown with the fewest assets. VMF-211's superb performance at Wake Island was made possible by hard-working, innovative, pilots and ordnancemen who adapted 100-lb Army bombs to Navy racks. Despite almost no training in dive bombing, the 'Leatherneck' aviators sank a Japanese destroyer and damaged a light cruiser before the island garrison was over-run.

Once the FM-2 arrived in numbers, CVE-based Wildcats possessed a significant strike capability with the 3.5-in high-velocity aerial rocket (HVAR). Capable of carrying three under each wing, an FM-2 possessed nearly the equivalent of a destroyer's broadside, effective against bunkers and many warships. However, the HVAR's rapid ballistic drop after rocket burnout posed serious problems in sight alignment, requiring fairly close firing ranges.

THE APPENDICES

COLOUR PLATES

1

F4F-3 white F-1, flown by Lt Cdr Paul H ('Hubert') Ramsey, Officer Commanding VF-2, USS *Lexington*, 7 May 1942
This aircraft was used by Ramsey to achieve his first two kills – two Zeros downed on 7 May 1942 (he claimed a third as a probable). It is unusual in retaining the tiny national insignia well back on the rear fuselage, a larger design by then being in widespread use. Ramsey claimed a Bf 109 (actually a Zero) on 8 May, with another as a probable. He later became the CO of Carrier Replacement Group 11. VF-2 scored 17 kills, all on 7/8 May 1942. Like most aircraft operating in the combat zone, this F4F-3 has had its fuselage code abbreviated from 2-F-1 (indicating the second-fighter unit's-first aircraft) to remove the squadron identifier.

2

F4F-3 BuNo 3976/white F-1, flown by Lt John Smith ('Jimmy') Thach, Officer Commanding VF-3, USS *Lexington*, 10 April 1942
On the outbreak of war, VF-3 had only ten F4F-3s (plus one borrowed from NAS San Diego) of an intended establishment of 18, having converted from the Brewster F2A-2 during August 1941. A 1927 graduate of the Naval Academy, Jimmy Thach had joined VF-3 as gunnery officer in June 1939, leading the successful team which won the Fleet gunnery trophy for VF-3, before becoming XO and finally squadron commander in December 1940. This aircraft was flown by Thach on 20 February 1942 when he and his wingman shot down a Kawanishi flying boat shadowing the carrier task force, and by Lt Noel A M Gayler when he shot down a G4M later the same day. Thach shot down a G4M himself while flying F-13 and damaged another on 20 February. This aircraft was decorated with three Japanese flags and the distinctive 'Felix the Cat' insignia of VF-3. It also has the high camouflage demarcation common on early non-specular blue grey/light grey aircraft, and the code number repeated on each side of the cowling, as per standard US Navy regulations. This combat veteran was finally lost while serving with VF-2 during the Battle of Coral Sea.

3

F4F-4 BuNo 5093/white 23, flown by Lt Cdr John S Thach, Officer Commanding VF-3, USS *Yorktown*, Midway, 4 June 1942
VF-3 re-equipped with F4F-4s at Kaneohe Bay in Hawaii in May 1942, passing its F4F-3s to VMF-212. It then embarked aboard the USS *Yorktown* for the Battle of Midway. Thach had, however, lost his pilots to VF-2 aboard the ill-fated *Lexington* and had to basically reform the unit from largely new and inexperienced ensigns, to which was added a core of experienced pilots from VF-42. In direct contrast to Jimmy Flatley's retention of the six-aircraft division (with three two-fighter sections), Thach preferred a four aircraft division as the primary tactical unit. In developing tactics for his squadron, and the Navy as a whole, Thach emphasised defensive tactics, advising against initiating attacks unless you held an altitude advantage. His leadership of 'Fighting Three' earned him a DSM. Thach used this aircraft to down three Zeros, and a new F-1 to destroy a torpedo bomber (and claim another as a probable) later the same day, bringing his tally to six confirmed kills and a probable. This aircraft was pushed over the side of the crippled *Yorktown* on 6 June to reduce top weight in an effort to prevent her from keeling over and sinking.

4

F4F-3 BuNo 4031/white F-15, flown by Lt Edward H ('Butch') O'Hare VF-3, USS *Lexington*, 20 February 1942
'Butch' O'Hare claimed five Mitsubishi G4M1 Model 11 'Bettys' of the 4th Air Group Air Striking Force during the Battle of Bougainville, all in a single mission and while flying this aircraft, with a sixth claimed as a probable. O'Hare gained two more kills in F6Fs but was killed in action in November 1943. VF-3 scored some 36 kills with the Wildcat at Bougainville and Midway. This historic aircraft had initially served with VMF-211 and survived the devastating attack on Oahu. After service with VF-3, it was passed to VF-2 and was one of only six F4Fs from VF-2 to survive the Coral Sea battle, taking refuge on the *Yorktown*. It was then passed to VF-42 and ended its days on 29 July 1944 when a pilot from MAG-23 wrote it off.

5

F4F-3 BuNo 3986/white F-13, flown by Lt Edward H O'Hare, VF-3, USS *Lexington*, 10 April 1942
Flown by O'Hare for the historic photo mission with Thach on 10 April 1942, F-13 had seen extensive action during the Bougaineville campaign. On 20 February, for example, it was flown by both Thach and Lts Noel Gayler and Lee Haynes, with Thach scoring 1.5 kills. The F4F wears standard markings for the period, with red and white rudder stripes aft of the main hinge line only, and with medium sized national insignia. The red rudder stripes and central 'dot' were removed from 15 May 1942, while white codes were more slowly replaced by black from late 1941. It was lost while serving with VF-2 at Coral Sea.

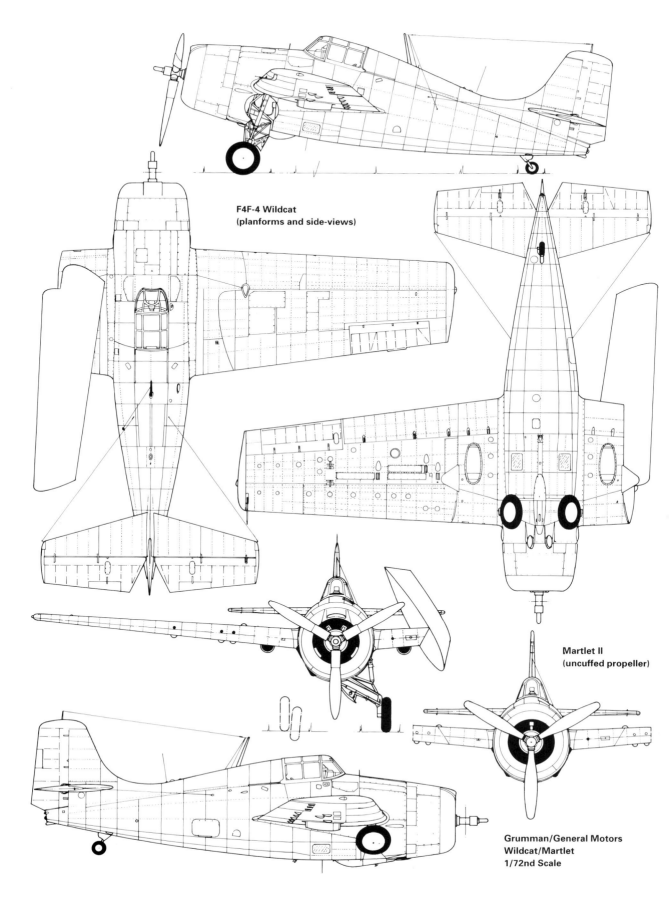

F4F-4 Wildcat
(planforms and side-views)

Martlet II
(uncuffed propeller)

Grumman/General Motors
Wildcat/Martlet
1/72nd Scale

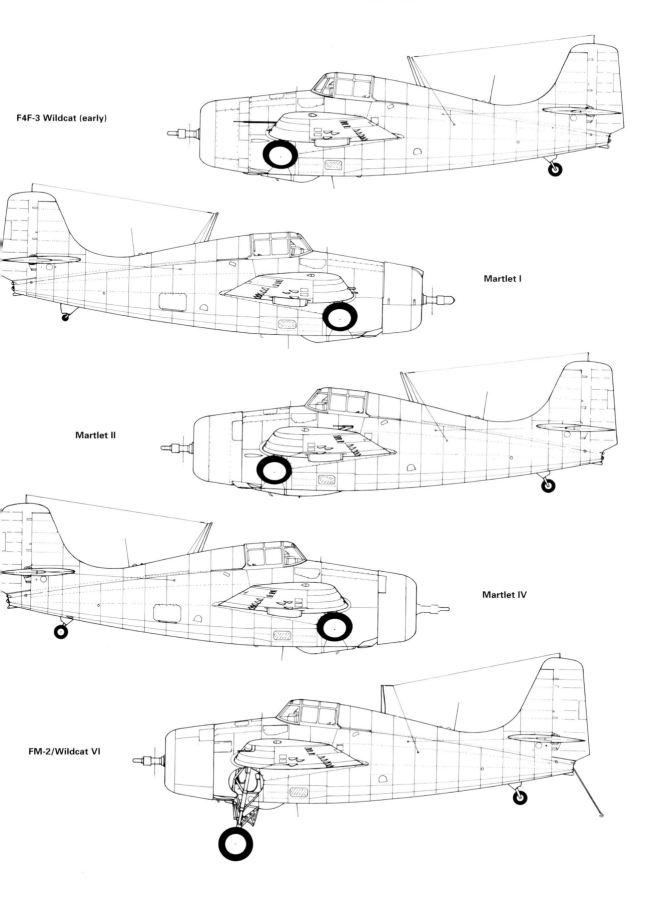

F4F-3 Wildcat (early)

Martlet I

Martlet II

Martlet IV

FM-2/Wildcat VI

6
F4F-4 BuNo 5192/black F12, flown by Lt James Julian ('Pug') Southerland, VF-5, USS Saratoga, 7 August 1942
Southerland used this aircraft to shoot down the first two Japanese aircraft of the Guadalcanal campaign, launching from the USS Saratoga. After downing a pair of enemy bombers, he was himself shot down by PO1C Sakai Saburo of the Tainan Air Group. The aircraft was formally stricken on 30 September, more than a month after it was lost! Southerland had to wait until 1945 when he (by now a Commander) downed a pair of 'Tonys' and a Zeke. VF-5's Wildcats were unusual in retaining the F code designator for longer than other squadrons, and in applying nicknames in black below the canopy rail. F-12 actually belonged to Ensign Mortimer C ('Junior') Kleinmann.

7
F4F-3A BuNo 3916/white 6-F-5, flown by Ensign James G Daniels, VF-6, USS Enterprise, 7 December 1941
This aircraft displays the markings worn by Fleet Wildcats on the outbreak of war, with a small star, full white squadron-role-aircraft code and no rudder stripes. Daniels escaped being shot down by US AAA on the first day of war, a fate which befell five other VF-6 F4Fs! He never made ace, but did share in the destruction of one aircraft (being officially credited with 0.33) and was credited with the probable destruction of 0.33 of another machine. His unit – VF-6 – was more successful, however, counting among its members two Wildcat aces – Lt(jg) Lee Mankin with five kills and Ensign Donald E Runyon, who later added three F6F kills to his tally of eight scored while flying F4Fs.

8
F4F-3A BuNo 3914/black F-14, flown by Lt Wilmer E ('Bill') Rawie, VF-6, USS Enterprise, 1 February 1942
In this F4F Bill Rawie scored the Navy's first kill of the Pacific War, downing a Mitsubishi A5M4 flown by Lt Kurakane Akira of the Chitose Air Group over the island of Taroa in the Marshall chain – he gained a further 0.33 of a kill on 4 June 1942.

9
F4F-4 BuNo 5075/black 20, flown by Machinist Donald Eugene Runyon, VF-6, USS Enterprise, 24 August 1942
One of the US Navy's top-scoring enlisted Naval Aviation Pilots (NAPs), and originally one of the 16 'Fighting Chiefs' of VF-2, Don Runyon scored eight kills with VF-6. He added three more to this tally after his promotion to Lt(jg) and service with VF-18. This aircraft was built at Long Island and delivered to the Navy on 10 February 1942, being assigned to VF-6 on 1 April. It participated in the Tokyo Raid and the Battle of Midway, and was transferred to VF-5 on 25 August, with whom it became black 38. It was destroyed by enemy bombing at Henderson Field on 15 October. The aircraft carries the LSO stripe on the port side of the fin, intended to allow Landing Signal Officers to determine the F4F's attitude on approach.

10
F4F-4 white 18, flown by AP/1c Howard Stanton Packard, VF-6, USS Enterprise, August 1942
Aviation Pilot First Class Howard Packard scored two damaged, one probable and one kill with VF-6 during June-August 1942. One of ten NAPs transferred to 'Fighting Six' from VF-2 in March 1942, he later won a DFC. Packard's aircraft was unusual in VF-6 in having white codes and in being decorated with victory symbols in the shape of small Japanese flags.

11
F4F-4 black 9-F-1, flown by Lt Cdr John Raby, VF-9, USS Ranger, Operation Torch, November 1942
Aside from the distinctive yellow ring around the national insignia applied for Operation Torch, this F4F-4 otherwise wears standard markings. Most of Raby's pilots were extremely inexperienced, many having less than 25 carrier landings. Unfortunately for them, they came up against some highly experienced French fighter pilots, some of whom had even been aces during the Battle of France. Moreover, the Curtiss Hawk 75 was more agile than the F4F-4, and the Vichy French had the advantage of flying over their own territory. Nevertheless, Torch proved a relatively inexpensive training ground for the F4F pilots. Raby himself downed a Leo 45 and a Curtiss Hawk, claiming a second Hawk as a probable.

12
F4F-4 BuNo 03417/white 19, flown by Lt Stanley Winfield ('Swede') Vejtasa, VF-10, USS Enterprise, 26 October 1942
Vejtasa scored three kills while serving with VS-5 during May 1942, and added 7.25 more (plus a probable) during his time with VF-10, seven of the latter score being downed in a single mission on 26 October!

13
F4F-4 BuNo 5238/white 14, flown by Ensign Edwin Lewis ('Whitey') Feightner, VF-10, USS Enterprise, 30 January 1943
'Whitey' Feightner amassed four confirmed kills and a probable during his service with VF-10, downing three 'Bettys' in this aircraft on 30 January 1943. During a second tour of duty with VF-8 in 1944 (flying the F6F) he added five more kills and a probable. Unusually for an Enterprise-based F4F, this aircraft lacks an LSO stripe.

14
F4F-4 white F21, flown by Lt(jg) William Nicholas Leonard, VF-11, Guadalcanal, June 1943
During earlier service Leonard had found the performance of the F4F-4 marginal with the new 58 gallon underwing tanks, describing the aircraft as a 'Dog' when flown in this configuration. He scored two kills with VF-42, two more with VF-3 and added a pair of Zeros on 12 June 1943 with the VF-11. His F4F is seen as it appeared on that day, with five victory flags and a tiny 'Sundowners' badge below the cockpit. Retention of the F role designator in the code was extremely unusual as late as June 1943.

15
FM-2 white 17 of VF-26, USS *Santee*, October 1944
Non-specular blue grey topsides and light grey undersides gave way to overall dark gloss sea blue from March 1944, with markings in insignia white. This FM-2 has silver underwing tanks, which seem to have remained more common than blue until the end of the war. VF-26 used a pair of narrow white bands across the fin tip as its unit marking, applied in white. Lt Cdr Harold Funk scored a single victory while flying with VF-23 on 8 September 1943, and added six more on 24 October 1944 whilst with VF-26, bringing him ace status.

16
F4F-4 black 41-F-1, flown by Lt Cdr Charles Thomas Booth II, VF-41, USS *Ranger*, early 1942
Charles Booth's F4F-4 wearing the full red and white rudder trim used until May 1942, with full codes in black and outsize national insignia. Unusually the aircraft does not wear the Boar's head insignia of the 'Red Rippers' which was applied beneath the windscreen of many squadron aircraft. Booth commanded VF-41 during *Operation Torch*, claiming one Dewoitine D.520 of the unit's total tally of 14 kills. Wildcat successes were marred, however, by the destruction of two RAF aircraft – a PRU Spitfire (identified as a black Bf 109) and a Hudson (claimed as a LeO 45).

17
F4F-4 black 41-F-22, flown by Lt(jg) Charles Alfred ('Windy') Shields, VF-41, USS *Ranger*, *Operation Torch*, November 1942
Although his Silver Star citation and official kill listings record the destruction of only two aircraft by Shields during *Torch*, other sources indicate that his score may have been as high as four. After shooting down a D.520 he attacked a pair of Hawks that were threatening a wingman, downing one and leaving the intended victim to polish off the other. He then destroyed a further Hawk, and shot down a Douglas DB-7 as it took off, before being shot down and forced to bail out. A further kill (of a 'Tony') scored with VF-4 in November 1944 may have brought Shields up to full ace status.

18
F4F-3 BuNo 2531/black F-2, flown by Ensign Elbert Scott McCuskey, VF-42, USS *Yorktown*, 8 May 1942
This Wildcat was used by Scott McCuskey (who had earlier shared in the destruction of a four-engined patrol aircraft) to gain his first full victory – a Zero from the carrier *Shokaku* during the Battle of the Coral Sea. Low on fuel, McCuskey landed aboard the damaged *Lexington*, where his aircraft remained as the ship burned, exploded and sank. McCuskey himself enjoyed a longer career, moving to 'Fighting Three' and reaching a total of 6.5 Wildcat victories, plus a further seven kills while flying Hellcats with VF-8. His F4F score included three 'Vals' destroyed when 12 Wildcats tackled 18 dive-bombers hell bent on sinking *Yorktown*. Despite splashing 11 Aichis, CV-5 was hit three times, causing mortal damage. The carrier was later sunk by a Japanese submarine.

19
F4F-4 BuNo 02148/black 30, flown by Lt Cdr Courtney Shands, VF-71, USS *Wasp*, August 1942
Shands destroyed five enemy aircraft in this machine, strafing them in a predawn strike against Tulagi on 7 August 1942. He added another ground kill to his tally, but was unable to open his scoring against aerial targets.

20
F4F-4 BuNo 02069/white 27, flown by Ensign George Leroy Wrenn, VF-72, USS *Hornet*, 26 October 1942
Wrenn used this aircraft to destroy five torpedo bombers on 26 October, landing back on the damaged *Enterprise* after the *Hornet* was itself crippled. His eventual tally was 5.5, and he never repeated his success of 26 October. Wrenn's F4F went on to VF-10 and was then returned to the USA for overhaul in May 1943. It ended its days with operational training command.

21
F4F-4 black 29-GF-10, flown by Ensign Bruce Donald Jacques, VGF-29, USS *Santee*, *Operation Torch*, November 1942
The CO of VGF-29 at *Torch* was Lt John Thomas 'Tommy' Blackburn, who was later to win fame as the leader of the F4U-equipped VF-17 – he was already an experienced carrier aviator at this early stage in the war. However, during *Torch* his leadership proved insufficient for his unit to gain more than a single kill, gained by the lowly Ensign Jacques over what he took to be a 'Bloch 174', but which was, in fact, a Potez 63.

22
FM-2 triangle 7, flown by Lt Leo Martin Ferko, VC-4, USS *White Plains*, June to October 1944
Martin Ferko accounted for four of VC-4's twelve kills, downing a pair of Zeros on 24 October and a pair of 'Jills' the following day. This FM-2 wears an unusual finish, more common in the Atlantic (where VF-4 scored the USN Wildcat's only two victories against German aircraft) with non-specular blue topsides and white undersides.

23
FM-2 white B6 *MAH BABY*, flown by Ensign Joseph D McGraw, VC-10, USS *Gambier Bay*, 24 October 1944
Wearing the snorting seahorse insignia and 'B' identity code of VC-10, McGraw's FM-2, with his name below the cockpit and the name *MAH BABY* on the cowling, also wears three Japanese flags representing his first three kills. The two kills which brought him to ace status were scored while he was attached to VC-80 following the sinking of the *Gambier Bay*.

24
FM-2 black 4, VC-13, USS *Anzio*, April 1945
April 1945 saw a brief period of success for VC-13, whose pilots accounted for eight enemy aircraft, with two probables and a damaged. A Zero and a 'Val' fell to Lt(jg) Doug Hagood on 6 April whilst serving with this unit – he also claimed a 'Val' as

damaged. This FM-2 may have been an emergency replacement rushed out to the Pacific theatre, since it still wears North Atlantic colours.

25

FM-2 white 29, flown by Lt(jg) Hatherly Foster III, VC-93, USS *Petrof Bay*, April 1945

Several VC squadrons operated aircraft with distinctive unit identification markings, and those of VC-93 were among the most attractive, with an outline shamrock repeated on the fuselage and upper surface of the starboard wing. VC-93 enjoyed a six-day period of success, downing 17 aircraft, four of which fell to the guns of Hatherly Foster.

26

F4F-4 black 29, flown by 1st Lt Jefferson Joseph DeBlanc, VMF-112, USMC, 31 January 1943

With a total score of nine victories (plus a single probable), one of which was scored while flying the F4U, DeBlanc was the Marines' 11th highest Wildcat ace. He completed his F4F tally by downing five aircraft in a single day – 31 January 1943. Low on fuel, and with his F4F badly damaged, DeBlanc was forced to abandon his aircraft at little more than treetop height, but was spotted bailing out close to a Japanese-held island by coast watchers on a nearby (friendly) island and was rescued. His aircraft is typical of 'Corps F4Fs at the time, with non-specular blue and grey camouflage, large national insignia and a two-digit code in black, with no unit identification whatsoever.

27

F4F-4 white 84, flown by Captain Joseph Jacob Foss, VMF-121, USMC, October 1942

Joe Foss may have been the top scoring Marine pilot of World War 2. 'Pappy' Boyington scored 22 victories with the USMC, and claimed to have scored another six with the 'Flying Tigers'. The latter kills include 1.5 confirmed ground kills, and two confirmed aerial victories (for which he was paid), but records researched by Frank Olynyk (the expert on US aces) cannot confirm the other 2.5. Olynyk is punctilious in pointing out that this does not mean that Boyington didn't score them, only that they can't be confirmed. This would seem to put Foss, with 26 confirmed kills, at the top of the USMC aces list. This aircraft was used by Foss to down several of the 19 Zeros he destroyed during his Guadalcanal tour.

28

F4F-4 white 50, flown by Captain Joseph Jacob Foss, VMF-121, USMC, Guadalcanal 12 November 1942

Executive Officer to Major Leonard K 'Duke' Davis, Foss scored his first kill on 13 October 1942. Judged 'too old' for fighters, he was a natural 'shot', and this eventually led to the last of his many requests for transfer from a recce unit to be approved. Foss flew white 50 for several of his victories. On 12 November 1942, for instance, he downed two 'Bettys' and a single Zero to notch up numbers 20, 21 and 22. White 50 was entirely representative of Cactus Air Force F4Fs, with no personal or unit markings.

29

F4F-4 black 53, flown by Captain Joseph Jacob Foss, VMF-121, USMC, 23 October 1942

Foss used this anonymous-looking aircraft to shoot an attacking Zero off the tail of a member of his division on 23 October 1942, thus claiming his eighth victory. He had a great respect for the enemy, and is quoted as saying 'If you're alone and you meet a Zero, run like hell. You're outnumbered'. Foss' score of 26 confirmed kills made him the most successful pilot of the Guadalcanal campaign

30

F4F-3 black 8, flown by Lt Col Harold William Bauer, VMF-212, USMC, Guadalcanal September-November 1942

Bauer amassed a total of ten kills (plus a probable kill of a Zero) during the bitter fighting for Guadalcanal – one of them while attached to VMF-224, and four (plus the probable) while flying with VMF-223. The official USMC listing gives Bauer ten kills, including the probable which he himself refused to claim! He was appointed commander of all fighters on Guadalcanal on 23 September 1942, issuing the advice 'When you see Zeros, dogfight 'em!' The optimistic and aggressive Bauer, often known as 'the Coach' or 'Indian Joe', went missing in action on 14 November 1942, over Guadalcanal, and received his Medal of Honour posthumously. His F4F is unusual in having a white cowling lip.

31

F4F-4 BuNo 02124/white 77, flown by Lt James Elms Swett, VMF-221, USMC, 7 April 1943

On 7 March 1943, 67 Aichi 'Val' dive bombers, escorted by 110 Zeros, attacked US shipping around Guadalcanal. Seventy-six 'Cactus' interceptors were scrambled to deal with this massive raid, including a four-aircraft division led by Swett, a 22 year old who had yet to fire his guns in anger! Swett led his formation into a squadron of 15 'Vals' as they tipped into their attack dive from 15,000 ft, having to ignore concentrated friendly AAA aimed at the dive-bombers. Swett accounted for two 'Vals' in the dive, and nailed another as it pulled out. Four more fell as they attempted to egress the target area, the gunner of the eighth smashing Swett's cockpit canopy and hitting his engine. His damaged aircraft (already holed in the port wing by a friendly 40-mm AAA shell) didn't make it home, the pilot having to ditch after his oil-starved engine seized. Swett scored a further 8.5 kills (with three probables, and a quarter share in a damaged 'Judy') while flying F4Us.

32

F4F-4 BuNo 02100/black 13, flown by Captain Marion E Carl, VMF-223, USMC, Guadalcanal August 1942

Like many of the top-scoring Guadalcanal pilots, Carl enjoyed a generous slice of luck. Of 38 Marine pilots killed or wounded, eight were shot down during their first two days, and another nine were lost during their first week of operations. But it was not just the tyros who were shot down. Foss, Galer, Smith, DeBlanc and Swett were all shot down but survived to fight again, while Bauer, arguably the most talented Marine fighter pilot at Guadalcanal, was lost in action. Marion Carl was no exception, and was shot down in this aircraft on 9 September 1942, but quickly replaced it with another 'lucky 13'.

33
F4F-4 BuNo 03508/black 13, flown by Captain Marion E Carl, VMF-223, USMC, Guadalcanal September 1942
With little escort work to be done, and with frequent appearances by Japanese carrier-based fighters virtually over their home airfield, the Cactus Air Force enjoyed all the traditional advantages of the defender and had a target rich environment, allowing big scores to be built up. Marine pilots claimed 395 kills between 20 August and 15 November, with VFs-5 and -10 adding 45 more, for the loss of 101 F4Fs. In reality the Japanese lost about 260 aircraft, but even this represented a kill:loss ratio better than 2.5:1, and ensured eventual victory. Only a handful of US pilots were productive, but those who did build up large tallies. Carl, for instance, scored 16.5, to which he later added two while flying F4Us.

34
F4F-4 white 2, unit and pilot unknown, USMC, Guadalcanal September 1942
Kill tallies were rarely painted on Marine F4F, it being felt that such decorations would generate unwelcome attention from the enemy. There were exceptions, especially during the brief periods when photographers from *Stars and Stripes*, or other propaganda sheets, were touring the frontline – this machine was duly decorated and photographed during one such visit.

35
F4F-3 white MF-1, flown by Major R E Galer, VMF-224, USMC, Guadalcanal September-October 1942
Robert Galer's F4F-3 is unusually colourful, with its red cowling lip and fuselage stripe. Thirteen flags appear below the cockpit rail, representing Galer's total official USMC tally, although individual unit records show a total of 14 kills. At least one of his aircraft wore the name *'Barbara Jane'* on the nose. During September and October 1942, Galer amassed 14 kills and three probables, including seven confirmed victories over the Zero, and this total, achieved only on the F4F, made him the fourth top-scoring Wildcat ace.

36
Martlet I AL254/R, flown by Sub-Lt Eric Brown, No 802 Sqn, FAA, HMS *Audacity*, 8 November 1941
Eric Brown, later famous as a test pilot (flying an unparalleled number of different types, including most captured enemy aircraft) and as the leading carrier aviator (with 2400 carrier landings) in the Fleet Air Arm, first encountered Grumman's latest fighter when Martlet Is were 'acquired' by No 802 Sqn at Donibristle in early 1941. He scored a victory on 8 November that same year, claiming the destruction of a KG 40 Fw 200. The Martlet I was an unusual aircraft, intended for French *Aéronavale* service, but with no provision for carrier operation, and with metric instruments.

It also had a 'pull to accelerate/push to decelerate' throttle, which was soon modified by the British to operate in the 'right' sense. The aircraft were diverted to the RN after the fall of France, and were fitted with four wing-mounted 0.50 cal guns in place of the 7.62 mm Darne weapons originally specified. They were powered by a Wright R-1820-G205A Cyclone engine, driving a Hamilton Standard propeller, because the F4F-3's Pratt & Whitney R-1830 was not then cleared for export.

37
Martlet I BJ562/A, flown by Sub-Lt Parke, RNVR, No 804 Sqn, FAA, Skeabrae, Orkney, 24 December 1940
On Christmas Eve 1940, Lt Carver and Sub-Lt Parke sighted a Ju 88 over Scapa Flow shortly after taking off after a suitably festive, lunch. They gave chase and eventually put an engine out of action, thus forcing the bomber to crash land in a field. The aircraft wears standard FAA fighter camouflage and national insignia, with a sky blue recognition band around the fuselage similar to those applied to all British fighters during the period.

38
Martlet III AX733/K, flown by Sub-Lt W M Walsh RN, No 805 Sqn, FAA, Western Desert, 28 September 1941
No 805 Sqn was a constituent part of the RN Fighter Unit which operated alongside RAF squadrons in the Western Desert during 1941 and 1942, operating with the Hurricane-equipped Nos 803 and 806 Sqns. The Martlets scored victories against three Savoia Marchetti SM.79s, a single Ju 88 and a Fiat G.50. The latter was downed by Sub-Lt W M Walsh, flying this Martlet III. Originally painted azure blue overall, the unit's Martlets soon picked up stone upper surfaces to camouflage them against the desert. The Martlet III was also used by No 806 Sqn, which claimed four kills when it escorted the *Operation Pedestal* convoy to Malta during August 1942, flying from HMS *Indomitable*.

39
Wildcat V JV573, flown by Sub-Lt R A Fleischman-Allen RN, No 813 Sqn, FAA, HMS *Vindex*, February 1945
Formerly F Flight of No 1832 Sqn, which formed flights of four Wildcat Vs for service on escort carriers, No 813 Sqn's Flight augmented units equipped with the Swordfish and Fulmar aboard HMS *Campania*, and then HMS *Vindex*. During early 1945 the unit's pilots shot down three Ju 88s, one of these falling to Fleischman-Allen, who had also shared in the destruction of an Fw 200 in December 1943, whilst serving with No 842 Sqn. The Martlet (later Wildcat) V was identical to the FM-1, and was likewise built by General Motors, although the FAA continued to refer to the aircraft as a 'Grumman'. This aircraft is by no means unusual in lacking identification codes.

40
Wildcat (Martlet) IV FN135, Sub-Lt R K L Yeo RN, No 819 Sqn, FAA, HMS *Activity*, 30 March 1944
Another composite squadron was No 819, operating a mix of Wildcats and Swordfish from

HMS *Activity*. While escorting convoy JW58, on 30 March 1944 Yeo shared a Ju 88 with Lt J G Large, while unit pilots accounted for two Fw 200s and a Bv 138 over the next three days. Yeo moved to No 816 Sqn aboard HMS *Chaser*, with whom he downed a Bv 138 on the last day of May 1944.

41
Martlet II AM974/J, flown by Sub-Lt B J Waller RN, No 881 Sqn, FAA, HMS *Illustrious*, Madagascar, May 1942

One of the most successful Martlet pilots, having a hand in the destruction of three enemy aircraft, Waller opened his scoring with a Potez 63 on 6 May 1942, shared with Lt Bird. The next day he downed two Morane MS.406 fighters, sharing one with Sub-Lt J A Lyon and the other with Lt C C Tomkinson, who downed a third single-handedly.

42
Wildcat VI JV377/6-C, flown by Lt Cdr Bird RN, No 882 Sqn, FAA, HMS *Searcher*, 26 March 1945

Lt Cdr Bird, who had earlier helped Waller down a Potez 63 while serving with No 881 Sqn in May 1942, led his unit in the last productive FAA Wildcat operation of the war – he claimed one of the four

III./JG 5 Bf 109Gs downed by his formation during a sweep off Norway on 26 March 1945. A mix of numerals and letters were common in FAA Wildcat/Martlet codes, sometimes with three digits, sometimes with only two. The last digit was always a letter, and was the individual aircraft identity.

43
Martlet II FN112/0-7D, flown by Lt Dennis Mayvore Jeram RN, No 888 Sqn, FAA, HMS *Formidable*, *Operation Torch*, 9 November 1942

Although not the top-scoring Martlet pilot, Jeram was the only FAA ace to fly the aircraft, adding his two Wildcat victories to a probable and four kills scored while seconded to the RAF's No 213 Sqn – equipped with Hurricane Mk Is – during the Battle of Britain. Flying during *Operation Torch*, over and off Algeria, Jeram claimed a 'Potez 63' (actually a Bloch MB.174 of GRII/52, Vichy Air Force) on 6 November, and shared in the destruction of a German-flown Ju 88 on 9 November with Sub-Lt Astin. His aircraft wears a US-style star painted over its roundels, and has even had the legend 'U.S.NAVY' applied to the rear fuselage. It does, however, retain the traditional crest of No 888 Sqn superimposed on the fin flash.

FIGURE PLATES

1
VMF-224 boss Maj Robert E Galer is shown in his standard issue USMC summer service uniform in late 1942. He has a set of gold navy wings pinned to the left breast of his tunic, above two rows of ribbons that include the Medal of Honour.

2
In marked contrast to Galer, Capt Joseph J Foss is depicted in January 1943 on Guadalcanal wearing 'fighting garb'. This consists of a 'suit/summer/flying', utility cap, adorned with the 'Corps globe and anchor badge, and Marine 'boondocker' boots. The leather patch on Foss' suit has been embossed in gold with Navy wings, rank and 'USMC' titling. He is carrying an AN-H-15 helmet, goggles and a life vest. His pistol belt supports a M1911A1 .45 cal pistol, first aid kit, ammo pouch and canteen.

3
Wearing a dark blue Royal Navy service uniform, with a matching heavy wool turtle neck jumper and standard issue Mae West, Sub-Lt Eric 'Winkle'

Brown of No 802 Sqn was dressed for comfort and warmth aboard HMS *Audacity* in late 1941. His headgear is also RAF standard issue, with the addition of smaller, but wider, US headphones.

4
Top-scoring FM-2 ace Lt Ralph Elliot of VC-27 aboard USS *Savo Island* in late 1944. He is wearing full flying gear including an AN-H-15 tropical helmet, goggles, US Navy 'suit/summer/flying', inflatable life vest, seat-type parachute with life raft, naval aviator's gloves and a Smith and Wesson .38 cal revolver and survival knife.

5
This Navy Lieutenant was attached to VF-21 in the Solomons in mid-1943, and he is wearing summer 'khakis', an A-2 flying jacket and khaki service cap

6
Lt(jg) E H 'Butch' O'Hare in January 1942, wearing the naval aviator's pre-war green/grey service uniform. Note the rank badges worn on the cuffs and collar, and the 'bullion wings' on the left breast.

BIBLIOGRAPHY

Brown, D *Carrier Operations in WW II. Vol. I: The Royal Navy.* US Naval Institute Press, 1974

Foss, J and Simmons, W *Flying Marine.* Zenger Publishing, 1979

Hess, W N *American Fighter Aces Album.* American Fighter Aces Association, 1978

Lundstrom, J B *The First Team.* US Naval Institute Press, 1984

Lundstrom, J B *The First Team and the Guadalcanal Campaign.* US Naval Institute Press, 1994

Miller, T *The Cactus Air Force.* Harper and Row, 1969

Olynk, F *USMC Credits for Destruction of Enemy Aircraft*

in Air-to-Air Combat, WW II. Privately published, 1981

Olynk, F *USN Credits for Destruction of Enemy Aircraft in Air-to-Air Combat, WW II.* Privately published, 1982

Robertson, B *Aircraft Camouflage and Markings 1907-1954.* Harleyford, 1964

Sherrod, R *History of Marine Corps Aviation in WW II.* Armed Forces Press, 1952

Sturtivant, R *British Naval Aviation: The Fleet Air Arm, 1917-1990.* US Naval Institute Press, 1990

Tillman, B *Wildcat: The F4F in WW II.* Nautical and Aviation Pub Co, 1983

Y'Blood, T *Hunter-Killer.* US Naval Institute Press, 1983